One-Up Strategies Business Schools Don't Teach

By
Dr. Gilda Carle

ACKNOWLEDGMENTS

Thank you to all
who generously shared your career experiences.
They made these One-Up Strategies come alive.

Dr. Gilda

Gilda-Gram®
Beware!
The situation you see
is never the total situation
that exists.

CONTENTS

INTRODUCTION

As a management consultant for Fortune 500 companies, corporations sought my counsel when thorny issues affected their bottom line. Sometimes, executives were surprised to hear their problems were interpersonal, because they had wasted money and effort on intricate reorganizations, revamped policies, and executive changes. By the time I was called in, the problems had usually gotten worse.

It was my job to winnow the wheat from the chaff, and report to the governing powers what the issue *truly* was. An issue we see is never the issue that exists. In each situation, after finding the problem, my next job was to propose how the company could solve their issues before they self-destructed.

One Fortune 50 company on Wall Street was having problems with its customer service personnel. The executives of a division were distraught as their bottom line plummeted. In meeting with the customer service department, I learned how disempowered they felt. I returned to their director and told him I would create sequential Lunch-and-Learns for this group. These would stretch over ten weeks. I boldly promised that by the time the program ended, his staff would feel much happier about themselves. Certainly, I knew this was not "corporate speak." But I also knew what I knew.

The director squinted and sternly leveled his eyes at me. He growled, "I don't care about how happy these people feel." Not missing a beat, and with full awareness that I might be about to sabotage my future in this company, I rebutted, "Oh, yes you do!"

What happened between my assertive pitch and the director writing me a six figure check, I cannot say. But a few weeks later, there I was in front of his staff, training them in interpersonal strategies they had never heard about.

This division's bottom line immediately began to soar. A manager told me about one of her direct reports who had entered her office to give her an update. As she always did, the manager purportedly listened while typing on her computer, not looking up at the subordinate delivering the news.

It was just a few weeks into our training, but the direct report assertively said, "Mary, I need you to be looking at me while I give you the details you requested." Mary was shocked. She'd never heard anyone on her team assert herself this way.

Traditionally, the thought is that management training is for the underlings, not the upper crust. But I know that if we throw a pebble in the ocean, there will be a rippling effect. As the customer service staff became empowered, their bosses would need to change their own business be-haviors. Some of them complained, but the results paid off.

The impact of my work was so dramatic for this division's bottom line, other divisions in the corporation requested I create the same magic for them. My tenure at this company lasted years, and I'm still in touch with many of those people.

I was also a business school professor, now Professor Emerita. While my professorial colleagues in our undergraduate and MBA program taught courses with the standard textbooks, I did not. Instead, I scoured publishers' book lists to discover hidden secrets of business success that needed to be grasped.

Books like "Machiavelli," "The Art of War," "48 Laws of Power," martial arts books, and even my own best-selling mass market tome, "Don't Bet on the Prince!" punctuated students' required reading lists.

Personally, I never colored inside the box, even when I was getting my Ph.D. in Educational Leadership at New York University. Sometimes I got in trouble, and other times professors wrote me off as "crazy." But the work I do is for the people I touch. And the people I touch have penned amazing unsolicited testimonials that you can read on my website, **www.DrGilda.com.**

I am grateful to be doing this unique corporate healing, because corporate healing is personal healing, and who's to say which comes first? Each day, I expand into other arenas that need empowerment work. Recently, I created a non-profit company, Country Cures, that empowers Homeless Female Veterans. Unusually, our programs use Country Music to get our points across—and we're saving Female Veterans' lives, along with those of their children and communities.

Similarly, with the swelling numbers of young women experiencing date rape, dating violence, and even suicide, I created an empowerment program that is saving their lives, too. It's reflective of the mass market, as you can gather from its title, "Don't Lie on Your Back for a Guy Who Doesn't Have Yours." But this book has been so popular with young women, I also wrote its companion, "My Rants & Ramblings Journal." It contains 365 Gilda-Grams®, one for each day of the year, where young women can explore their empowerment expansion through sequential journaling techniques.

Contrary to what that Fortune 50 director believed before he met me, *Empowered people are happy people. Happy people are productive employees and emotionally healthy human beings!* Those are the only kind of people you want driving the bottom line.

I have impacted many groups, from youngsters to CEOs. I know that the real meaning of life is never in the lines, but *between* the lines—in the *people* who achieve the task for which a company must show profit. It is people skills that drive these profits. It is these people skills that we must nurture.

"One-Up Strategies Business Schools Don't Teach" was derived from corporate papers I wrote and delivered, my published CEO magazine articles, and my continued consulting work in corporate America. Today, I do keynote and motivational speeches, I conduct Lunch-and-Learns across the country, and I privately consult with executives and non-executives on my Advice & Coaching platform on DrGilda.com. In all, I am grateful to grow from those who seek me out, as much as

they say they grow from me.
Dr. Gilda

1

Your Reputation: "Wanna-Be" or "Will-Be"?

Finding the right path requires avoiding the wrong messages.

While mingling at a professional association to which I was about to deliver a keynote dinner speech, a woman excitedly shared that she had just taken a job after a miserable year of unemployment. She beamed that it had been a contact from this association that had connected her with her new employer.

As we chatted, a man joined in to hear the woman's good news. The man's response was surprising—and downright demoralizing. "That's an awful company to work for," he blurted out—as though he had even been asked. The people in the chat circle froze in silence. The woman became immediately depressed, and spent the remainder of the cocktail hour in isolation, drinking and chain-smoking.

Tough times have altered the rules of the traditional job search. Networking, more than resume distribution, accounts for a greater percentage of new job connections today. As more and more people link up through networks, how many are unwittingly projecting the negativity they are picking up around them?

Bad times can bring out the worst in people. Part of this is due to the way we've been socialized. By the time a person is 18 years old, he or she has heard 148,000 negative messages, calculated to be 22 negative messages a day! With this as our upbringing, it's easy to absorb the counterproductive cues that bombard us.

How much of the negativity around you are you allowing to penetrate your feelings and behaviors? This will depend on whether you take on a "Wanna-Be" or a "Will-Be" perspective. The good news is that you can actually get to choose.

Anatomy of a Wanna-Be

A Wanna-Be wants to be like the other guy who has the proverbial "greener" grass. However, a Wanna-Be never does a thing to make that happen. This person is cynical and pessimistic, and feels helpless in trying to control his or her life. Envy and jealousy permeate this person's character, so he or she lives to dispense put-downs and hurl brickbats at any ready target.

Anatomy of a Will-Be

A Will-Be is the actual person with the "greener" grass, who is always striving to make it still greener. A Will-

ONE-UP STRATEGIES

Be uses hard times to re-invent himself or herself, to create innovative niches, and acquire new contacts.

A Will-Be's spirit is entrepreneurial, with a strong and dedicated inner direction and focus. A Will-Be positively refuses to be affected by a Wanna-Be's sour attitude and responses. In winter, while Wanna-Be people freeze, Will-Be people ski.

When you meet a miserable Wanna-Be, be prepared. Hold firm to your Will-Be resolve. Understand that there are only two basic emotions that exist: love and fear. Wanna-Be people are frightened people, longing to be recognized, yearning to be loved. Don't let their negativity affect you, and bring you down. Will-Be people are secure in their abilities, they don't depend on others' approval, and they certainly love themselves. These are the personality types you want to be around.

You can either internalize a Wanna-Be's inner discontent, as did the woman I met at that cocktail party, or choose to secretly offer that nasty person kindness and healing—and then leave his or her midst.

Overcoming Wanna-Be negativity is one of life's many tests, particularly during tough times. Avoid being a Wanna-Be's target by remaining confident and unaffected. More than anything, allow your Will-Be attitude to attract Will-Be contacts that will enhance your life and upward mobility.

2

Resist Overfunctioning

Are You Pointlessly Absorbing Other People's Issues?

There is a popular game called "Overfunctioning" that many people unwittingly play. Do you recognize your-self in any of these scenarios?

- Bob is arguing on the phone with Bonnie. He hangs up and is furious. He vents to you, and then feels better. Two days later, Bonnie calls and YOU are cold to her, angry at how she treated Bob. Bob, however, gets on the phone pleas-antly, as though negative words be-tween the two had never been exchanged. YOU become enraged.

- Joe passes you in the hall and groans about a mistake he made on an important account. You offer to double-check his corrections, although you are already overextended this week.

- June needs your help on a project. You put your goals on hold, immediately coming to her aid, thereby unable to achieve your own work goals.

True to the nurturing female archetype, I spent a large part of my adult life playing this debilitating work game. Unbeknownst to me, by Overfunctioning for others, I was setting myself up to Underfunction for myself. The Underfunctioners whose work I took on never had to work out their problems, since they happily passed them on to me. As a result, I was forever exhausted. Moreover, by being the willing accepter, I unwittingly sent the message, "I'm capable, and you're not."

Underfunctioners are the people we blame for "just not getting it." But they actually "get it" pretty well, by habitually getting others to do their work. Their "learned helplessness" can range from, "Where do we keep the keys to the office?" to "How do I turn on this computer?" Underfunctioners can be our children who have difficulty separating from us, their parents, just as well as they can be our colleagues who can't seem to achieve anything in our absence.

Sadly, while the Underfunctioner gets someone to take on his or her chores, the greatest losers in this game are the Overfunctioners. *Taking responsibility for other's issues sidetracks us from taking a responsible role in our own.*

At the end of the day, Overfunctioners lack the energy to develop skills to make ourselves successful, or to get ourselves recognized or promoted beyond the current position we hold. In short, we trade up our own goals for the hope of being found to be indispensable.

William Oncken's classic article in the Harvard Business Review, "Management Time: Who's Got the Monkey?," likens our taking on other people's problems to placing *their* monkeys on *our* backs. Monkey-accepters are classic Overfunctioners.

If you recognize yourself as an Overfunctioner, decide whether you want to meet your goals and be respected, or be liked. If you are ready to make a change, follow these two steps:

1.   As soon as someone is ready to pass it to you, determine whether a "monkey" is rightfully yours.

2.   If you choose to accept a monkey as your own, decide right then what you intend to do with it once you have it. You will either need to feed it to nurture its growth, or need to remove it.

The Bible says, "Love thy neighbor as thyself." It does not say "instead of" thyself. Chronic Overfunctioners must learn to give from their *overflow,* not from their core. In other words, be sure to give from what you have *left over after you have nurtured yourself.*

There is an alternative to accepting other people's problems as your own; you can instead guide these people. When someone approaches you with his "monkey," say,

"That's a shame. What do you think you'll do about that?" This way, you're not offering to dedicate your resources to this person when you need them to sustain your own goals.

Monkey-refusal leaves the creature on the back of the person to whom it rightfully belongs. It also supports the emotionally healthy message that "I'm capable *and* you're capable, too."

There is nothing wrong with helping a colleague in need. We all do that when it's necessary. However, for chronic monkey-passers, you must ask yourself whether it's worth depleting the power you need to fuel your goals.

Ultimately, before you gain respect from others, you will need to show them how you respect yourself.

3

Handle a Hostile Audience —With Your Eyes

*Turn conflict into common ground
with the strongest weapon you have.*

Public speaking is the Number 1 fear for most people. But if you're speaking in front of a hostile audience, fear is certainly to be expected. Nobody wants to receive public persecution. Yet, when hostility confronts a speaker, it must be addressed. Otherwise, resentment builds, and with the slightest provocation, an entire audience can become unmanageable.

Many public speakers open their presentations with a prepared monologue—one that bridges the audience's agenda with their own. Others immediately immerse the audience in participative dialogue to build enthusiasm and activate involvement. But both monologue and dialogue heavily rely on words to get their meaning across. And because as little as 7 percent of our information is communicated through words alone, a speaker's best bet is to first communicate with facial and body expressions, particularly with his eyes.

Yes, before uttering a word, engage in what I call an "eye-alogue"—prolonged empathic eye contact with the person or people you're to address. More penetrable than monologue, and more disclosing that dialogue, eye-alogue can help establish rapport and cooperation—particularly among hostile parties.

Secrets Behind Eye-alogue

Former President Ronald Reagan used eye-alogue before he began each press conference. He looked reporters in the eyes—and then smiled and greeted them by name. This initial eye-alogue told his viewers, "I'm on your side." It promoted Reagan's reputation as "the great communicator." Similarly, Mikhail Gorbachev was considered by many to be one of the world's best speakers. Using his hands and voice together, he, too, first dominated a meeting with his eyes.

America focuses much attention on the eyes with attractive eyeglass frames, tinted contact lenses, lush false lashes, and colorful eye makeup. Our vocabulary-substantiates the richness of eye-alogue: *gaze, glance, glare, gawk,* and *gape* are just a few synonyms for "look." Because eye-alogue should precede dialogue and monologue, the wise communicator can use it to choose such appropriate vocabulary words and phrases.

The science of Neurolinguistics teaches us that "visual"

communicators look up before telling us they "see" our point of view; "auditory" communicators look from side to side before explaining they "hear" our side of an argument; and "kinesthetic" communicators look diagonally downward before admitting they "feel" we are right.

Thus, by noting the direction of a listener's glances during eye-alogue, a speaker can know to choose words that derive from *see*, *hear*, or *feel* to connect with the eye cues--and the person--before him. Based on the principle, "Like likes like," connecting a speaker's vocabulary to a listener's eye-alogue enhances subliminal interpersonal communication, even under the most hostile conditions.

Using Your Weapon

After your usual introduction, pause silently before the angry group that sits before you. Divide the audience into imaginary quadrants, and for 3 seconds each, 12 seconds in all, seek out friendly eyes among the faces. Have an eye-alogue with each of these—and then smile. Finally, take a deep breath and honestly acknowledge your listeners' fears: "By now the information of the XYZ report is out in the open. We will need more time to analyze the findings. Tonight, let's openly discuss our mutual concerns. I'll gladly fill you in on the facts we currently have."

By using eye-alogue to establish unity, you set the stage for believable dialogue. With each question from the audience, you can now offer a sympathetic monologue in response. When you're finished, conduct eye-alogue for another few seconds, and then smile to some friendly audience eyes.

Call upon a receptive face for an audience question. With subsequent queries, note each interrogator's eyes, and respond in visual, auditory, or kinesthetic terms: "I see what you are saying" (for a visual interrogator), "I can *hear* how upset you are" (for an auditory interrogator), and "I *understand* why you feel as you do" (for a kinesthetic interrogator).

If a hostile interrogator gets carried away, quickly disengage eye contact with this person, and engage in eye-alogue with another, more friendly audience member.

When used properly, eye-alogue can be the perfect prelude to a dialogue and monologue that contains your agenda. Note that this formula changes the usual tendency of speakers to begin with their prepared agenda and to monologue an audience to sleep. Especially with hostile listeners, eye-alogue establishes immediate rapport, and it can then be followed by dialogue and monologue with grace.

Now that you're armed with the arsenal to allay audience resistance, achieve your objectives exactly as you want, without being overrun by loud and hostile audience disrupters!

4

Ace Every Media Interview

Honestly assess your fear of failure,
but also your fear of success!

Your hands are clammy and your heart is racing as you sit across from an unfamiliar interviewer on national TV, trying to sell yourself and your brand. Or, the CEO of a Fortune 500 company begins probing your job history in his office—its successes and failures—when two of his associates walk in, sit down, and also begin to assess your performance. In both instances, you feel naked and awkward—but you know you must continue on.

You are not a lone contender. The world watched as the nation's highest-ranking experts marched into Trump Tower for the then president-elect to scrutinize them for a potential cabinet position. No matter how high their rank or how commanding their achievements, each was hard pressed to sell.

You know that only your worst enemy would try to sabotage this vital moment that you're fortunate to even have. But it is possible that as you sit before the arbiters of your future, you are unconsciously undermining your own chances of success.

Of course, no interviewee consciously thinks, "How can I self-sabotage?" But during times of stress, your self-worth is put to its toughest test. On some level, you may feel you don't deserve to be on this TV set, or even to be hired, particularly if you've just endured a humiliating media storm or a painful downsizing. So, you may unconsciously say or do something that takes you out of the running, before someone else does it for you.

If you're prone to negative thinking, even if it's only occasional, your mission now must be to reverse your self-defeating thoughts the moment they begin. It's your job to demonstrate that not only are you in command of what you're saying, but that you can also roll with the punches during such stressful times. In other words, no matter what, you must totally believe in yourself so much that it's evident to your assessors. And you can't fake this. As is said in show biz, the camera never lies!

Do You Fear Success?

Ironically, for many people, success feels as dangerous as failure, based on underlying feelings that they're not worthy.

They fear promoting themselves, partly because they've

been taught not to brag, and partly because they don't want to rise to a level that threatens their true self-doubts. Indeed, many TV interviewees and job candidates alike manufacture excuses for not succeeding in earlier situations. For example, "I didn't get enough sleep," "I had to go to a meeting just two hours before," or "The person hated me on sight" are common utterances.

Some saboteurs go a step further by placing themselves in the "If Only . . ." torture chamber. Their internal statements to themselves include, "If only I'd gotten my degree," "If only I had more experience," or "If only I were younger . . . smarter . . . better trained."

At the very least, excuses allow interviewees to blame their failures on something or someone other than themselves. Then they can rationalize that they're not failures after all, but people whose potential hasn't been fully recognized.

Unfortunately, media interviewees and job candidates most likely to make excuses are those most obsessed with the *look* of success. Because they want the trimmings so badly, they may come across as too aggressive, instead of projecting a classy air of confidence that resonates with audiences before them.

Steak vs. Sizzle

The higher the job level, the more important confidence is. It may be the credentialing steak that gets you onto the TV screen or in the door as a job candidate, but it's the confident sizzle that keeps your audience pumped to want to see and hear more.

Demonstrating traits of eagerness and willingness to listen help you project a confident image. During a job interview, casually presenting visual news articles or media interviews on your cell phone or tablet may convince an interviewer that you're the best candidate.

3 Steps to Confidence

Develop a "confidence fluency" that becomes a natural part of your personality. Like language fluency, learned confidence can be an asset in all areas of your profes- sional and media life. With obvious self-assurance, your prospects are likely to improve without having to lobby very hard.

Confidence fluency is a skill that can be learned. By using the 3-step formula that follows, you'll impress audiences—and get called back. These three steps are preparatory homework, before your actual appearance occurs.

1. Believe in Yourself

Recognize if and how you may potentially be sabotag- ing your goals. Honestly identify situations that cre- ate anxiety for you. Evaluate the behavior you project when you're on the verge of success to determine if you subtly undermine your goals.

Successful self-promoters believe they deserve to be where they are. Pattern yourself after the children's book, "The Little Engine that Could." The little engine was able to huff and puff up the great hill, because he told himself, "I think I can, I think I can."

Propel that reasoning a step further. Don't just tell yourself you *think* you can do something. Change that message to, "I know I will, I know I will." Strong self-belief is the basis for transforming your confidence into a self-fulfilling prophecy.

Challenge: KNOW that you have much to offer—and much to gain as you describe your talents to someone. KNOW that everyone who enters your life is a teacher, and that you'll learn a needed lesson before you progress to the next step. KNOW your efforts deserve reward, and prepare to graciously receive your payoff now.

2. Visualize What You Want

Perceive or visualize your goals as already having been achieved. Contrary to the old saying that seeing is believing, accept instead that "Believing is seeing." When you believe something is possible, you'll perceive its accomplishment.

A TV interview or a big job prospect may loom larger than life to you right now. But they aren't life-or-death sentences. Money is only a way of keeping score, a mistake is just another way of doing things, and you can learn more from what doesn't work the first time than from what does. There are no failures—only lessons in what to do next. Know your worth, and the payoff you deserve for it will come calling as soon as you're ready.

3. Achieve Your Goals

Achieve your interview plan with confidence. Practice risk-taking in relatively safe settings, as you derive honest feedback from friends and colleagues. Evaluate your assets and log your achievements. When circumstances get you down—and they will if you're breathing—review your logbook. Honor these achievements by giving yourself rewards you planned in advance.

<u>Challenge:</u> Focus on your past efforts at self-promotion, and list your three greatest accomplishments. Identify what went right. Create a flow chart of what you did at the beginning and how you followed it to completion. Which people did you impress? How? Reread this list before appearing on air or before a job interview. Reviewing all you've positively done will surely boost your feelings of competence.

When learning any new skill, maintain your confidence by following these 4 steps:

1. Critique your confidence level often on audio or video.

2. Apply your new skill in front of as many different audiences as possible.

3. Cope with the criticism that normally accompanies changes in behavior.

4. Rehearse, rehearse, rehearse.

Observe successful people you know or those you see in the media. Note the certainty with which they walk and talk. Many of them had to LEARN this level of self-promotion from professionals such as I. Doing homework way before an upcoming appearance gives you an edge before you actually perform. However, be on your guard, because nothing goes as planned.

Many times, I've appeared on TV to discuss one topic, only to find that the discussion goes in a different direction. Because I am psychologically prepared and emotionally psyched, I am never shaken by any turn of events, even on live television.

You can achieve the same level of comfort when you face people who are judging you. Slay the dragon of your fears. YOU'RE in charge.

5

Pledge to Benefit in Bad Times

Do you seek pleasure
or simply the avoidance of pain?

Is where you are in life where you want to be? If the answer is "No," that's good. There are only two forces that motivate us: moving toward pleasure and moving away from pain. Of the two, it is the desire to avoid pain that motivates us most. Yet, that is the force that also brings us to our subsequent successes. Pressure drives our actions as much as it transforms jagged rocks into sparking diamonds.

A Vice President of a company now being downsized was bemoaning the state of his troubled organization, and feared for his job. His body language revealed hopelessness and a diminished spirit. It was 9 AM on a Monday morning. That was his usual dreaded day and time over the past several years, but now it had escalated to sheer terror. I warned him that this is when the majority of heart attacks occur.

Sure enough, one Monday morning, he displayed a panic attack so intense he had to be rushed to the hospital. While he didn't actually go into cardiac arrest, his symptoms mimicked a serious condition—which frightened him all the more.

If you are suffering the stresses of life, embrace this feeling and acknowledge that your discomfort can motivate you to take your next more positive step. Create a Mind Map. Here's how. Draw a circle with your name in it. Let your thoughts flow to your fingers.

As words come to mind, write them in separate circles around your name—but keep switching from your dominant hand (your conscious mind) to your non-dominant hand (your unconscious mind). Draw arrows to show which words result from the words before them.

Because your words encircle your name, rather than run down the page, your mind can make associations it would not ordinarily make during traditional linear writing. You will see a pattern to your innermost feelings, especially the ones you had never thought about before.

The Vice President's pattern showed positive words closer to his name, and negative words further away. He recognized how he perceived that positive situations became negative ones when he thought further about them, and he acknowledged that these thoughts were bringing him down.

This man spent the next week Mind Mapping in this way. He set out to chart his feelings each day, and then he moved to charting his goals. Since this exercise challenged both his conscious and unconscious mind, I was not surprised to hear the nightmare he had on a Sunday night before his usual Monday morning bout of anxiety.

My client described his dream as seeming to last the entire night. In it, he fought demonic creatures that were attacking him and spewing malodorous green bile into his face. He screamed out, "You're not gonna get me," as he awakened in a cold sweat. Yet, he remembered he had managed to kill every demon with his bare hands!

The next day, for the first Monday in years, the Vice President felt energized. His Mind Map began with positive words, and this time continued with other positive words extending from them. Some words further away included "ready," "action," and "make it happen." The man was amazed.

After only a week of examining his discomfort, this man had fought the demons on his dark side—and won. His attitude changed completely—and everyone he worked with noticed. He made lunch dates to network in his organization, and called for meetings to motivate his troops. He became one of the few positive leaders left amid the doom and gloom. He called me to gloat about being offered a new top position in his rapidly changing company. Apparently, despite the downsizing and all the fears that accompanied it, the people at the top now saw this man as too valuable to lose.

Your pain can work for you—as long as you acknowledge it, see where it's leading, and decide you are willing to change your thoughts. Mind Mapping allows you to articulate your feelings so you can release them and exchange them with more positive emotions and results.

Once my client let go of negative feelings, he was free to formulate lofty goals he had never considered before. Somerset Maugham said, "It's a funny thing about life: If you refuse to accept anything but the best, you very often get it." The secret is in knowing how—and now you do!

6

Build Big Deals
from Small Talk

Take only 3 steps

to optimally mix business with pleasure.

Party talk can be the springboard for important associations. Would any executive consider attending an important meeting unprepared? The "business party" (an oxymoron) is a meeting, too, though it masquerades as a relaxed and informal get-together. Be careful! Too many biographies tell of such informal occasions that unwittingly altered people's futures forever.

Business parties require networking skills that can turn small talk into big deals. But there are factors working against even the most able small talker. For one thing 7 seconds is usually as long as your listener will tune you in before tuning you out. That's probably enough time for you to announce your name, company, and position—if you speak quickly.

The problem is that your words only comprise 7 percent of the power you project. They are competing with your body language (55 percent of your image) and your vocal tones (38 percent of your image). Your listener may not even be paying attention to that simple, vital utterance—your name.

How do you beat the odds and leave the event with an image that others will want to pursue? Networking is a science. It involves 3 sequential networking steps that can readily build those big deals from your seemingly insignificant utterances. That is, if it holds your listener's interest beyond the mere 7 seconds. Unbeknownst to most, small talk requires the same type of preparation as any important meeting.

Step #1
Know your strategy.

Develop a plan before the affair occurs. Prepare answers to 3 questions:

- What is my goal for attending the event?
- Who are the power players I want to meet?
- What is the impression I want to leave?

Every one of your business events must be evaluated according to a future payoff. Ask in advance about the size of the party, the dress code, and who will be attending. This paints the picture of decorum you will want to adapt.

Generally, **fit in—but stand out.** Knowing the who, where, and why is the first part of your homework. You will then be able to study information about people you want to get to know better. Contrary to popular belief, knowledge is power—ONLY if you can use it to your benefit.

After you have established your goal for attending the party, fine tune questions for those you want to target.

You also want to dress and act in accordance with the impression you want to leave. Your objective before the party is to learn about your audience. Your objective at parting is to get them to remember you and want to contact you later. I call these the two R's: to be Remembered and to be Referred.

Step # 2
Know how to build rapport.

After doing your homework and discovering key information about those with whom you want to develop a relationship, exchange non-personal pleasantries with the specific guests you have sought. Also with those guests, pool the common interests you have unearthed, and open channels for further communication. To encourage more than simple, one-word responses, ask open-ended questions beginning with "How?," "Why?," "In What Way?" and "What?"

Step #3
Know when the party's over.

As much fun as you may be having, remember that this is a BUSINESS event. As such, you are there to impress and project your unique charisma and power. Keep remembering that your goal is to be sought after later.

Never overstay your welcome. Less is more. Leave the event with mystery so your contacts will want to meet you again. If you were successful in building big future deals from your seemingly insignificant small talk, you'll need a good night's sleep to respond to all the follow-ups you'll receive the next day.

7

Ignite a Networking Mindset NOW!

Don't let your innate fear of reaching out cripple you.

Everyone eventually realizes that only they can take responsibility for their future success. But it usually takes time and some painful experiences before they do. Industries and careers change rapidly, and companies no longer promise womb-to-tomb caretaking. Most people hold a succession of jobs during their careers. Even self-employed professionals recognize they aren't guaranteed lifetime victory unless they remain on top of their game.

But just as you need cutting edge skills to topple the competition, you must also employ "Connection Power" to make smooth transitions upward. The time is now to scope prospective referrals for your next move. You can't afford to wait to network until you're unemployed.

Too Withdrawn to Start?

The concepts of "career ownership" and networking are often frightening. Fear keeps many people stuck in intransigence. Almost everyone—from entry-level employee to corporate president—feels some fear in reaching out. Often, fears are camouflaged by excuses, such as being too busy or not believing in the value of the process.

For example, during a Team Communications workshop I ran at a Fortune 100 company, many upper-level bankers complained about being passed over for promotions. When I asked, "What have you done to promote yourself?," they said they didn't feel self-promotion was necessary.

Some people don't know where to start. Others don't know what they want to do next. When I asked a group of my graduate business students what they intended to do with their MBAs, most said they had no idea.

Many employees are still mired in the belief that someone—a recruiter, family member, or boss—will intercede on their behalf and find them the perfect job. When they're asked about their strategy for getting ahead, they don't have an answer. Unfortunately, the reality is that most people will never "be discovered" unless they take action.

The Rules of Networking

To develop your Connection Power, realize that a network isn't a bank where you withdraw favors when you're unem- ployed. Recently, this misconception led

many professionalst to arrange bogus "information interviews" with busy corporate managers. Instead of conducting research about an industry, they only asked for jobs, causing their contacts to feel deceived and used. After that, it was impossible to regain
access to these busy insiders.

There's a big difference between asking for a job and developing an ongoing, mutually supportive network that you and your contacts continually tap into. In a mutually supportive network, you don't sound self-serving when you ask for feedback about a company. For the best networkers, this adage rules: "What you give out, you get back."

Seize the Moment

If you're a reluctant networker, step up your efforts now. Ironically, one of the best times to make contacts is immediately after starting a new job.

Your network should include not only the people in your list of contacts, but also past business associates, long-time friends, and others who helped you get where you are today. Have you remained in touch with these people from your past? This is very easy to do using social media.

My own career changed drastically because of contacts I've made through networking. I had created a free monthly newsletter with advice about projecting a Power Image™, a concept I devised for business professionals. I sent the newsletter to 1,000 people each month, not knowing what to expect.

When I was first beginning my career, I received a call from a newspaper that wanted to hire me to write a monthly column on this topic. I didn't know the person who called, and I have no idea how he even got my newsletter. The column attracted the attention of a local TV station producer, who suggested I turn the advice into a few public service announcements for the Home Shopping Network. I was happy to do that.

After taping several 5-minute segments offering tools for succeeding in life, I began receiving calls from producers of major national talk shows who had previously rejected me as an expert guest when I cold-called them. As a result of those 5-minute segments, that year alone, I appeared on more than 100 news and talk shows, thus jumpstarting a career on national TV. That, in turn, led to my signing a book deal for $1 million.

All from a free newsletter that was sent out at my own expense, with only a wish and a prayer!

When you begin networking in earnest, you'll see that the world is really quite small. Following the notion of "Six Degrees of Separation," only six people separate us from anyone else. But don't stop networking after you've met your six new contacts.

You never know who knows whom. You also never know if a certain someone will change your life! You'll never know for sure—unless you keep your networks going.

Don't try to make networking a new approach to finding a job. It should become your way of life!

8

Win Work's Battles and Wars

Instead of going to war, go to strategy
—and enhance your success.

Belittled by his boss in front of his colleagues, a manager retaliated with obscenities. A few months later, he was fired. Raging over a nasty highway dispute, a trucker hurled expletives, drove a few yards, and slumped over his steering wheel with a heart attack.

These two different men in different environments engaged in separate battles using streetflighting counterblows. Both learned that revenge was sweet—but only in the short run.

Streetfighting catches up with its users. A desperate struggle for a quick return of fire can be damaging—or deadly. Is winning a battle worth losing a war? Battle "wins" create battle scars. It's not unusual for an alleged winner to limp away while the loser awaits the chance to get even. When an injured party looks to get even, the problem often gets worse.

The 1,500-year-old book used by American troops in the Persian Gulf was "The Art of War." A less-known translation of its title is "The Art of Strategy." Author Sun Tzu's objective was to avoid war whenever possible by carefully applying martial arts strategies. The martial artist *responds* in strength, rather than *reacting* in weakness. The strategy consists of 3 steps:

- Planning

- Observing

- Letting Go

1. PLAN your goals. Decide to invest your energies only in winning these goals. Winning is possible especially when your attacker is off guard and there is limited interference.

2. OBSERVE your attacker's tactics, especially those that make him or her weak and unguarded. Plot the best time to make your move.

3. LET GO of the desire for revenge. Letting Go is not cutting yourself off from your emotions; it's realizing you can't control or change anyone but yourself. Step out of the path of your attacker, and allow your assailant to assail himself or herself.

I was being interviewed by an aggressive TV talk show host who kept cutting into my sentences and responding to callers' questions directed at me. My topic was "How to Manage Anger," and my PLAN was to talk about anger, not become an angry woman retaliating against a disrespectful

TV talk show host. On live national television, I planned to project a soft sell with a strong shell, no matter what was transpiring.

I OBSERVED my host's rude interruptions, and consciously decided to LET GO of my desire to react. Instead, I smiled in strength whenever I could get a word in. The public isn't blind to disrespect.

When I returned to my office, I received calls and emails praising my professionalism, and blasting my host's disrespect. It was interesting to me how others noted the host's aggressions, and how they also waited to see how I would comport myself.

Too many people around us today are happy to instigate a battle, misbelieving their "fight" will show their strength. But just because *they* choose the dance of rage does not mean that we must dance with them.

If you feel the need to retaliate, consider this: Hostility has more to do with coronary illness than the proverbial Type A, overwrought, overworked personality.

There's no payoff in going to war. Instead, go to strategy. Plan, Observe, and then, Let Go. You will promote your longevity, your power, and your success. That's how to win each battle and win every war.

9

Increase Your Network's Net Worth

Benefit from big payoffs with Connection Power.

What is the net worth of your network? Many small business owners join professional networking groups to increase their net worth. Members are expected to attend regular meetings and provide contacts. To avoid competition, some organizations allow only one business in each field to join.

Although entrepreneurs have traditionally joined civic and trade organizations to make contacts, it was always under the guise of providing social outreach to their communities. These days, it is de rigueur to join an organization for the abiding purpose of making business connections. Finally, it is no longer a secret that Connection Power is directly proportional to net worth.

Networking for its own sake is not a new concept. A successful executive client of mine boasted, "There are only 1400 people in my world. I can get to any one of them with just a phone call." He certainly proved his Connection Power when he phoned one person in his network, who phoned a second, who phoned a third—who offered him a large business loan.

You may or may not agree with the number 1400, but it's worth the effort to take inventory of your current net worth.

Determine your Connection Power

Complete the following Net Worth Analysis.

1. Divide a sheet of paper into 3 columns:
    Column 1: Significant Others
    Column 2: Friends
    Column 3: Business Associates

2. Quickly list as many people as you can in each column.

3. Label every name you've listed as one of the following:
    Maintainer (one who helps you do your job effectively)
    Propeller (one who pushes you into new areas to help you advance)
    Drainer (one who sucks your energy dry)

The Net Worth Analysis is a revealing instrument. What did you discover?

One vice president discovered that most of his Significant Others, Friends, and Business Associates were Maintainers. From the Net Worth Analysis, he realized that in order for him to get promoted to president of his bank, he needed to surround himself with more propellers. After we discussed it, he reset his networking with that goal in mind.

A sales executive found that her three Significant Others were Propellers who pushed her more than she could bear. In fact, they pushed her so hard, they became Drainers! From her Net Worth Analysis, she found that the people closest to her were providing her with too much pressure in her life, which became counterproductive to her sales efforts. She planned to let her Significant Others know that their goals for her were not the goals she held for herself.

A CEO found his Business Associates were also his closest friends. He knew that his business life had become overwhelming, but he couldn't figure out the reason. After completing his Net Worth Analysis, he pledged to create more separation between his professional life and his personal life.

And then there was I. Some years ago, the name at the top of each of my 3 lists was the same person. He had been my Significant Other, best Friend, and Business Associate. Few names followed his, demonstrating how isolated I had allowed myself to become. In fact, my entire network consisted of about 5 people in all.

A ravaging divorce spun me into the realization that having a naked network can devastate a person as well as a career. It took me considerable time and work to lengthen and strengthen each of my 3 Net Worth columns. I had learned a valuable lesson from my own Net Worth Analysis, one which I carry with me today.

We continue to grow and develop as human beings. As a consequence, our Net Worth Analysis must always be updated. A monthly assessment of your 3 columns can provide a gauge of your progress, but take action NOW. By intensifying your Connection Power, you'll unwittingly be increasing your net worth.

10

Hone Your Image

Be sure your image is helping your career.

The image you project is what people reflect when they communicate with you. Your audience perceives the way you feel about yourself, and treats you accordingly.

Do you know how others perceive you? To find out, take the Image Projection Test.

Draw a picture of yourself as an animal. This is not an exercise in zoological accuracy; the only element that counts is your perception of the animal's characteristics. Answer each question below without lengthy contemplation:

1.   Why did you choose this animal?

2.   Is this animal more predator or prey?

3.   Is it sociable or solitary?

4.   How does it relate to other animals?

5.   What gives it pleasure?

6.   How would other animals perceive this animal's personality?

7.   Think of the one person you would most like to add to your network. Draw this person as another animal. Respond to the same questions above for this second animal.

Gerry Smith, CEO of a small manufacturing firm, drew himself as an eagle. When asked to respond to the above questions, he noted that he chose the eagle because of its power and perspicacity. (He proudly described himself as "eagle-eyed" in his company, as well as in his industry.) He noted that the eagle was a predator of smaller birds. He smiled when he described its independence, noting that it usually displayed no interest in befriending other animals, and preferred to be alone.

"What gives the eagle pleasure," said Gerry, "is its broad wingspan that allows it to fly far and high. Other animals are fearful of this enormous creature." The CEO carefully punctuated his responses with pride in having chosen such a powerful identity.

For the person he wanted in his network, Gerry chose Sam Jones, publisher of one of the major manufacturing magazines in the country. Gerry believed that the publisher could give his company much needed exposure in upcoming issues. That would significantly increase Gerry's corporate revenues.

As Gerry began to draw Sam as an animal, he found himself illustrating an elephant. Gerry thought of Sam as a person who never forgot key information and important people. He described an elephant as neither predator nor prey, but as a good-natured, sociable sort that ate peanuts and basked in the sun.

When I asked Gerry to think of how an eagle and an elephant would relate, he furrowed his brow and replied, "I guess they wouldn't interact at all. The eagle is independent, and the elephant is social. The eagle is malevolent, and the elephant is benevolent. But even with their differences, the eagle would gain from the sources of information and contacts the elephant never forgets."

I asked, "What would the eagle offer the elephant in return?" Gerry had to admit that if the elephant were fearful of the eagle, their relationship would deteriorate.

From the Image Test, Gerry discovered that in order to connect with Sam, he would have to shed some of his independence and be more open to socializing with him. He also recognized that since fear does not generate trust, he would have to modify his predatory demeanor. Gerry and I are working on the image he projects to all his other networks, as well.

Nobody wants to network with predators. Yet many networkers mistakenly believe the people they meet are there merely to do them favors. Beneficial networks require interaction on equal footing, where both parties can feel they are each reaping rewards.

Think of the animal you chose for yourself. Is it a giver or a taker? A mover or a shaker? As you network, establish ongoing rapport *before* you request a favor. In this way, you will not be perceived as a predator who is only interested in his own personal gain.

The image you give out is the image you get back. I can personally attest to the power of this technique. For my animal, I chose a million dollar racehorse. A few years later, long after I remembered even doing this exercise, I secured a book contract for a million dollars!! For sure, what you project, others reflect. It may take a while for all to gel, but it definitely does happen. It's never too soon to launch your projection of power.

11

Pitch Your Hardest Sell

Create 30 well-planned seconds for a lasting impression.

You can build more networks in 30 seconds than you can in 30 minutes! In only 30 seconds, commercials in the media advertise 3 basic points:

- What a product is
- What a product does
- What's In It for Me? (WIIFM?)

The objective of all marketing campaigns is two **R**'s: to be **R**emembered and to be **R**eferred. Simple!

Chief executive officers make speeches routinely. But a 30-minute speech may not be as effective as a properly executed 30-second "commercial" they make on themselves. This is not a slick promo for some product. No, this commercial is much more difficult; it calls on someone to sell himself in an "elevator pitch," where there is little time from the elevator's opening to its closing.

Thirty seconds is really the paltry amount of time any of us have to make a killer impression a listener won't forget. To be unforgettable, you'd better gift-wrap your goods.

In the media training I conduct, executives discover that a 30-second pitch to sell themselves is excruciatingly long! Truly, *the more we say, the less people remember.* And in a culture where people process only 25 percent of what they hear, and remember a measly 10 percent of that, *less is always more.*

The 30-second sell always includes a "hook" that's an attention-grabber your audience won't forget. Your audience may consist of one person or thousands, as long as your hook makes an impact. "Ho Hum," says your audience. "What's in this information for me?"

What's in it for your listener is, at first, mostly non-verbal. "Non-verbal?" you ask. "With all the effort I put into writing my words?" Yes, sorry, but 55 percent of the impact you make when you're in front of someone depends on the image you project.

Manage your listeners' perceptions easily by projecting 3 C's:

- Consideration
- Credibility
- Control

Consideration is the sincerity that boasts your polished expertise. One executive used jargon specific to her industry, but outsiders found her difficult to understand, and rated her as arrogant. A corporate president chose to lean back in his chair, with his arms behind his neck, in an effort to appear casual. When we played back his video image, he himself noted how condescending and inconsiderate he seemed.

Headhunters tell us that 7 out of 10 people lose their jobs not because of lack of skill, but due to personality conflicts. Communicating Consideration for others can promote you faster than a slick resume.

Credibility conveys likeability. People do business with people they like. And since people like people like themselves, you will be more credible if you subtly mirror the postures and gestures of your listener. A potent tool for building rapport, this technique is also used effectively by researchers working with primates in the wild. Credibility draws people toward you, which is the result you seek.

Control is your body energy saying, "I take my work seriously, and I take myself lightly." It is emitted through your posture, facial expressions, gestures, and voice. During his 30-second "commercial," one CEO muttered, "My name is Joe Doe. I am president of uh (and he cleared his throat), uh . . ." He ran out of time before quickly hitting the 30-second mark.

When we watched the video, he admitted how insecure he appeared. We discussed his uncertain vocal tones, his downcast eyes, and his stiff posture. Two weeks later, he declared bankruptcy. His emotional bankruptcy had shown long before his legal woes were publicized. This CEO's lack of Control over his body energy sabotaged the networking he needed to do during his stressful transition time. Your Control is a dead giveaway of your power—or lack of it.

Carefully rehearse your image on video and audio. Hire a professional who understands the nuances of image management. Since this is all about YOU and your FUTURE, it's certainly worth your investment!

Now onto the verbal "hook." This is your opportunity to be catchy and intriguing. Ask yourself, "How will my hook benefit my listeners? "Will it make them richer? Smarter? More successful?"

Your audience wants to get answers to these questions. Sum up their payoff in one statement or captivating phrase. This is your promise to your audience members who want to know whether to invest their time listening to you.

I spent years as the relationship expert on the Sally Jessy Rafael TV show. On one show, I discussed one of my motivational speeches called "Commando Tactics for Business People." In disbelief, Sally said, "Commando Tactics?" When I repeated the term back to her, my hook had already been restated at least three times on national television. That kind of advertising is fantastic!

Because I had already projected the 3 C's, the audience laughed with us, as Sally chided me over this title. I knew we were all in sync, and now the audience was so intrigued, they were anxious to hear more. You will always know when you've hooked your listeners.

Every person you meet provides another opportunity for your "commercial." Be armed to advance it when the timing is right, without hitting your listener(s) over the head.

After you've carefully Considered their readiness, demonstrate your personal Credibility and Control. Your audience is constantly assessing whether yours is the image they would want to Remember and Refer. Success will be seen immediately if the person asks to see you again. It's exactly the same as dating!

12

Engage this Unique Networking Formula

Consider to whom you're speaking!

Executive job seekers finally have a heightened awareness of the need to network. "Who you know" is the most important factor in nailing a new position, behind the use of search firms and recruiters.

The problem is, many job seekers are stuck in old habits, and use conversational techniques with the standard monologue and dialogue they believe will make an impression.

Traditional monologue and dialogue rely only on words. People process only 25 percent of the words they hear, and remember only 10 percent of those. Would you like only 10 percent of your carefully chosen words to be remembered?

Moreover, the impact people make through their conversations is 93 percent dependent on non-verbal cues—not on those precise words you painfully prepared. So, focusing only on the words you speak is clearly the wrong approach to be Remembered and Referred—the two goals you're after.

The language of our bodies accounts for 55 percent of how we come across. Therefore, the networker should concentrate on the first part of the body the listener sees: the face, and particularly, the eyes.

Before you engage in endless monologue, or try to strike up a dialogue, engage what I call "eye-alogue," steady and empathetic eye contact. More penetrable than monologue and far more intimate than dialogue, eye-alogue immediately establishes harmony and rapport.

Our culture focuses great attention on the eyes, with flattering eyeglass frames, tinted contact lenses, lush false lashes, and dramatic eye makeup. Words such as "gaze," "glance," "glare," "gawk," and "gape" emphasize how vocabulary substantiates the richness of eye-alogue.

Former President Reagan began each news conference with eye-alogue by looking reporters in the eyes—then smiling and greeting each by name. This initial eye-alogue communicated, "I am on your side." And it promoted his reputation as "the great communicator."

Reflecting Reagan's powerful communication skills, I recommend executives take an acting class. Executive clients who follow this suggestion thank me for all they learn from basic acting techniques.

Most people demonstrate a predisposition for one of three styles of communicating: visual, auditory, or kinesthetic (feeling). The wise communicator can "read" her conversational partner's style, and mirror that style and vocabulary when it is his or her turn to respond.

While we can buy in any language, when we sell—and that's what we are *always* doing—we must sell in the language of our listener. Communication that is not understood is not communication at all.

This is how it works. You approach someone with some information you know he will find valuable. The science of Neurolinguistics teaches us that "visual" communicators look up before telling us they "see" our point of view. "Auditory" communicators look from side to side before explaining they "hear" our side of the argument. And "kinesthetic" communicators look diagonally downward before admitting they "feel" we are right.

Using the cues you receive from eye-alogue, respond with, "I see what you are saying" for a visual speaker. For an auditory speaker, offer, "I hear how enthusiastic you are about that idea." For a kinesthetic speaker, reply with, *"I understand why you feel as you do."*

Based on the principle that "like likes like," patterning your vocabulary after the speaker's eye-alogue allows you to go with the speaker's flow and be heard. This bonding also builds trust.

When your listener trusts you, he or she will listen more intensely to what you have to say. He will ask you specific questions about yourself and your work. You have primed him, and now you're ready to delve into a monologue boasting your skills. This is how you can count on your listener to be more receptive.

This foolproof networking formula, then, consists of eye-alogue first, dialogue second, and monologue last. Things have certainly changed from years past, when monologue first was the rule of thumb, followed, perhaps, by some meaningless dialogue.

Lao-tse, author of the oldest book of Taoism, wrote, "To attain knowledge, add things every day. To attain wisdom, remove things every day." You get to choose between knowledge and wisdom. Are you ready to let go of the past to let in the riches that will promote harmony in your new networks?

13

Use Your Power
—Or Lose Your Power

Use what you've got,
or someone else will get it!

Not too long ago, I escorted a powerful patron of the arts to a private dinner party. The ambiance was that of gourmet elegance. All the guests were stars in the world of theatre: finely schooled, extensively traveled, and multilingual. The mix consisted of the right ingredients for an equal exchange of power. Right? Not necessarily. As it turned out, the network did not work because of a few indiscretions committed by the host.

It started on a promising note. As preparation, my companion's secretary had called in my name in advance. This is an important practice. Names are our most cherished identities. By calling ahead, the host avoids bein embarrassed by mispronouncing or misspelling a name. In most social encounters, names are frequently not listened to at the onset, and consequently not remembered during the function.

The guests at this party knew the requisite name repetition technique to enhance the recall factor: "How do you do, Gary." "Grace, it's so nice to meet you." Name repetition reinforces the auditory memory, and injects the routine rhythm of conversation with a complimentary sound of one's individual stamp.

So far so good. On to the dinner—and on to the first mistake. My companion's place card put him to the right of the host of the party. **Power Tip #1: In any power game, the person to be solicited is seated to the left of the host.** The custom dates back to ancient times, when the host found it easier to stab the opponent on the left with the dagger in his usually dominant right hand. The guy on the left held the power because it was clear he was important enough to be feared as an enemy and subject to attack.

To be seated to the host's right is to be assigned the role of "nobody." Safer, perhaps, but not noteworthy. Thus, this seating arrangement gave my companion all the power of the ancient medieval guest who survived the dinner.

Since the host wanted to solicit my companion's financial support for the theatre company, the host needed to be in control. He therefore should have taken his "rightful" place to the right of the patron.

I was placed to the immediate right of my friend. This confirmed my own unimportance to the group. **Power Tip #2: To play the power game, also play to the benefactor's accompaniment.** In an intimate gathering such as this, the hosts might have guessed that the patron would bring some one he was proud of.

But even if he had ushered in someone less than savory, both the patron and his accomplice should have been wooed. A host never knows the power an escort may have over his targeted guest. Tsk, tsk.

Wine was poured and the room's decibel level rose. The laughter became raucous as some of the guests began to lose their inhibitions in full view. **Power Tip #3: Never drink so much that you lose control.** People may have a short memory for your name, but they never forget your inebriated antics.

The president of the theatre company sat opposite me at the table. At first, his conversation scanned politics, public figures, and pâté. But as the drinks flowed, he began to make inappropriate advances toward me. **Power Tip #4: Never, never, never solicit the wrong person for the wrong thing!** If these people were trying to win a friend and influence his purse strings, they certainly had not studied the manual on panache.

The final segment of the evening was capped when some neckties emblazoned with the theatre company's logo were handed to most of the male guests. The key word here is "most." *They did not give one to my escort—the person whose funds they were trying to solicit!!* **Power Tip #5: If you want to give the impression of inclusion, INCLUDE.** At least, if the host had given my partner one of the neckties, perhaps—if only out of guilt—my partner might have considered writing a check.

It was obvious what the host had wanted from my friend. But he did not play to the box seats. My escort came with the power, and also departed with the power. He had the dinner, he had the wine, he had the evening's conviviality, and *he kept his money in his pocket.*

Clearly, this network did not work. The ambiance was extremely elegant, but the host needed schooling in how to use, not lose, his power!

14

Get Face Time
Whenever Possible

Meet and greet with 5 deliberate steps.

Get in front of someone's face whenever you have the chance. If a person wants to sit down with you for a quick cup of coffee, jump at the chance. A staggering 55 percent of all impressions we make are determined by our face-to-face body language.

Significant people present themselves at the right time and the right place—but we can make a great impact if we're in front of their faces. When you get that chance, exude impressions of abandon and adventure: abandon of any fear of rejection, and adventure for meeting a new person to discuss new opportunities for you both. New is always exciting. And with an air of positivity, anything and everything you never felt possible can occur.

The best news is that people we attract are mirrors of what we ourselves project. Where we set goals, we carve boundaries; where we carve boundaries, we reap rewards.

Evaluate people you consider successful. Note the twinkle in their eyes and their readiness to laugh and have fun. I address life as a continuous costume party. The way people communicate in costume invites others to cavort at their celebration.

Who doesn't like a celebration? While my attitude is laced with levity, the meeting/greeting process, however, is a deliberate strategy of 5 distinct steps that follow in smooth succession.

Step #1: Small Talk. According to the Book of Lists, speaking in public is most people's Number 1 fear, even greater than the fear of death! *Conversation is public speaking in miniature.* Whenever we are selling ourselves, there will be some natural anxiety. The general theme of Small Talk is that you don't need to know as much as you need to ask. Asking questions that are open-ended, that require more than just one-word responses, prompts the conversational flow.

Step #2: Individualization. As much alike as we may seem, we must maintain our differences. The back-and-forth banter of Step #1 now escalates into discussing and revealing our unique characteristics. Having differences is positive; if people boasted identical viewpoints, there would be no need to interact at all. Yet, because of the variations, the crafty conversationalist must be careful not to set up a "You" vs. "Me" draw.

Step #3: ConFRONTation. Now that you have ac-knowledged your differences, you can choose wheth-er to work through them, or to get into heated debate. The ConFRONTation step invites participants to be upFRONT about their feelings as differences are dis-closed. It uses a simple, "When you____, I feel ____ " sentence construction. For example, "When you talk so highly about Carol's department, I feel you obliter-ate the accomplishments of ours." ConFRONT your partner with poise and grace. The listener will not feel defensive, since you are discussing your feelings, and each speaker will understand and respect the other's uniqueness.

Step #4: Trust. Now that people have conFRONTed each other in ways that can be received and venerated, trust will build. Trust evolves because of the richness of the differenes that have been acknowledged and ac-cepted. Trust is paramount in every relationship. And it is often the missing link in relationships that derail—whether business or personal.

Step #5: Collaboration. The people who make it to Step #5 embrace a philosophy of abundance. They weave intricate networks with others, because they ac-cept their uniqueness as special. They believe there are ample sources of opportunity and wealth. Jealousy and greed don't enter the scope of possibilities for them. Through giving and receiving, the new collaboration enhances its unified worth.

This 5-Step meeting and greeting strategy permeates all kinds of relationships. If it's followed with lightness in its seriousness, it will be a win-win, as your inital connections lead to others.

15

Strengthen Your Visibility Quotient

Discover how visible you are
to people you want to impress.

Recently, a vague acquaintance called. He was some-one with whom I had not spoken in many years. After our requisite and reciprocal small talk, he blurted, "Gil-da, I'm calling to network with you. Do you know of any jobs in my field?"

Totally clueless, this man had committed the most com-mon white collar crime known to business. He con-fused asking for a job with asking to tap into my ongo-ing mutually nurturing network. The former consists of requesting someone's benevolence; the latter is a per-quisite you ethically and legitimately earn.

Networks are not banks for the withdrawal of favors during periods of recession and unemployment. Instead, they involve ongoing give and take interchange during times when life is prosperous.

The people most successful at such affiliating volunteer and contribute *before* they need others' generosity. Then, if a need should arise, they probably have to do little asking for help, because the networks to which they were continually giving automatically jump in.

The willingness to give makes us visible in our company and industry and life. So goes the adage, "What we give out, we get back."

Surprisingly, the visibility that is so essential to solid networking is never dependent on position. A college president who never walked out of his office was fired by his board as soon as his contract expired. His key role was to raise the institution's endowments. But since this man had few contacts due to his being so contained, he was a poor fundraiser and leader for the school.

In contrast, at the same institution of higher learning, a secretary who won corporate awards for contributing to community charities was promoted to assistant vice president of the school as soon as a slot opened. Her visibility had been obvious and radiant.

How visible are you? Even if you currently have the job of your dreams, circumstances can change without warning. One super salesman's career derailed after the sudden death of his mentor.

In our fickle world, no one can afford not to increase his or her Visibility Quotient (VQ), because we never know which cards the game of life will deal us.

True success is determined by preparing for unforeseen opportunities. One key to being visible is to give of your time, talents, or money—without expecting pay-off.

Test your VQ by completing the following:

1.   In my *company,* 3 ways I increase my visibility are ____, ____, and ____.

2.   In my *industry*, 3 ways I increase my visibility are ____, ____, and ____.

Assign 1 point to each of the items, totaling 6 points in all. If your VQ score is 5 or 6, you are on the right track. Determine whether your contributions fall mostly within your company, your industry, or both. The appropriate concentration for you depends on what your goals are and where you want to go. An overall VQ score of 4 or less cautions you to look closer at how successfully you are heading toward achieving your objectives.

A vice president said she eventually wanted to become a technical writer. After getting a score of 0 on the VQ test, she realized she had been devoting all her time to accomplishing her work goals, and little time preparing for her future writing goal.

While she talked a good game, she had not tried to publish one column. Since she recognized this is what she wanted to do in years to come, she knew she had better start to raise her VQ in the writing arena.

The usual excuse to why someone is not making himself abundantly visible is, "I'm too busy doing the job for which I'm paid." For the sake of mental and physical health, everyone should be striving toward a balanced life of work and play. If you're not visible enough in an area in which you want to rise, parcel out some of your free time to pursue increasing that VQ score.

One corporate president voiced interest in helping the nation's homeless, although he never made the time to pursue that endeavor. Meanwhile, his company was bought by a large conglomerate, and he was dethroned. Within a month, a political appointment was being sought for someone to head a commission on the homeless, and this man could have been the perfect choice.

But he was never even considered, because no one knew of his interest in this case. Had he taken the VQ test earlier, he would have discovered that his commitment to his company's bottom line was only *one* element he should have been focusing on during his visible leadership reign.

Today, social media gracefully allow us to boast our achievements in full view. Since our visibility is continually out there, we can easily mold it to pave the way toward our future goals. There is no telling what lies ahead for any of us. But if you raise your VQ now, as you give, so shall you receive.

16

Know Your Handshake's Hidden Messages

The grip that holds your future is in your hand.

You are literally holding your business' future in your hand. For good reason, "Reach out and touch someone" was the theme of a telephone company for many years. The hand you offer an acquaintance determines whether a relationship will develop—and how.

The handshake is the most widely used form of greeting in the Western world. Originally, its ancient purpose was to show an associate that your right (and dominant) hand was free of weapons. The military salute developed for a similar reason. As the Industrial Revolution spread, the use of the handshake to make deals and seal business agreements extended itself into the social realm.

While the face has only 14 bones, each hand has 27. A hand can operate as a crowbar, a level, or a wrench. And it can reveal a caresser or aggressor. The Bible mentions the hand of God more than 1,400 times. We, ourselves, judge others as "high-handed," "even-handed," "heavy-handed," or "underhanded." We may be quick to point the finger of accusation, but we always want to keep our finger on the pulse.

Our fingers bend and stretch at least 25 million times during our lifetime. Because of this flexibility, handshakes have been named "the visible part of the brain," reflective of our self-esteem. Would you want to do business with a "limp fish"? Or, would you prefer to know that your business is being "well-handled"?

In an executive communications workshop I conducted, participants tested each other's non-verbal messages with their handshakes. One woman offered her hand flat against her partner's, with a grasp. She explained that she was tired of getting her ring fingers squeezed beyond blood flow. But her partner read her handshake as cold and disinterested.

In the same group, a man shook hands with a woman and proceeded to place his left hand over their clasp. While the covered handshake can be perceived as a show of warmth, this woman read it as a patronizing power play. In a moment's time, we second-guess our acquaintance and immediately determine the kind of touch to which he or she will best respond.

Bill Clinton once gave New York gossip reporter Cindy

Adams a lesson on handshakes:

"Your whole palm must slide all the way in. To the hilt. Far as it can go. So, your fingers are touching the other person's wrist. I have big hands, but Hillary has little hands. A big hand can harm her with a tight squeeze. I've taught her how to do this so her fingers don't get hurt or a ring doesn't cut into her. You actually lock your thumb inside the other person's thumb. This way you are in charge of the shake, your fingers are out of the way, up the other person's wrist, and the other guy can't harm you."

Would you have imagined so much thought could go into a simple handshake?

Evaluate the messages sent by your own handshake according to the following 6 factors outlined by David Lewis in his book, "The Secret Language of Success":

1. *Your hand's appearance*, consisting of the length and shape of your palm, fingers, and nails

2. *The texture of your grip*, consisting of the softness or roughness of your hands, as traditionally indicative of your work and social class

3. *The moistness of your hand*, which increases with anxiety.

4. *The amount of pressure used in your grasp*, ranging from bone-crushing to lifeless

5.   *Your handshake's duration*, around the average 5-second mark

6.   *Your style of grip*, whether palm down (dominant), palm up (submissive), or palm face-to-face (cooperative)

Your objective is to be Remembered and Referred in the ways you want. Practice a 5-second grip with different people and solicit their feedback. For hands larger than yours, per Bill Clinton's suggestion, spread your index finger and thumb to place you on a par with your acquaintance.

At social events, hold your drink in your left hand to avoid offering a cold and clammy hand impression. Finally, prepare to reach for business cards in a place where your hands can readily and gracefully retrieve them.

Before you "reach out and touch someone," be mindful that touch is a major part of the body language messages you send. If you make your touch memorable, it will promote your future success. All without uttering a single word!

17

Vow to Achieve
Your Wildest Goals

Successful goal achievement
requires living life ON PURPOSE.

Each day gives us the gift of 86,400 seconds. We can either spend our seconds wisely or we can totally squander them. People who achieve their goals deliberately structure their productive time around each of these 6 categories:

- Health
- Finances
- Self-Improvement
- Spirituality
- Family
- Social

For example, a person who works around the clock at his job, without exercising or ingesting good nutritional fuel, is likely to fall apart. So will a person who is devoutly spiritual, yet procrastinates in performing her necessary workload for which she is being paid.

Each of the 6 categories for thriving has a unique focus. Health goals include caring for our inner and outer housing. Financial goals include managing and maintaining our financial security. Self-Improvement goals include actualizing our potential, rewarding ourselves, receiving rewards from others, and enjoying time alone.

Spiritual goals include honoring and giving to others. Family goals include devoting time and activities to people who matter to us. Social goals include vacating our usual routine to explore new and playful adventures. If any one of these 6 categories remains unfilled for too long, our lives suffer from the imbalance. And when we're off balance, we eventually crash.

Chris had been downsized from his last job, and he was suffering a depressing and debilitating time. To get his mind off his woes, he began doing volunteer work while deciding which career goals he wished to pursue next. This lofty Spiritual choice made him feel great. But soon he found himself running out of money. It was finally time to find a paying career.

I asked Chris to initiate his career-seeking process by writing his first financial goal. He wrote, "I hope to find a job—and I'm worried about the economic condition of our country."

I told him, "I hope to find a job" is too vague, and the subject of the country's economic status is a diversion.

Sure, Chris' concern about the economy and its effect on people was a conscientious Spiritual goal for him, but he was already doing volunteer work, thus gaining Spiritual fulfillment. All the while, he still had not identified a financial goal for himself.

As I guided him through this exercise, he began to acknowledge that he was putting off the goal he really needed to emphasize. In addition, the other five goal categories remained relatively empty. We agreed on the need for redistribution of his energies.

When conditions seem too frightening and stressful, most people choose to concentrate on things that will divert their attention away from the issues at hand. But that does them no good.

I coached Chris to write an overall financial goal by using my "DESERVE" format along with specificity that would attract exactly what Chris wanted.

Chris thus began to structure his statements along these lines: "I DESERVE to find a marketing job within 6 months that pays at least $90,000." I counseled him to write that goal in 25 different ways each day, sharpening it, shaping it, identifying the industry he wanted, the location he wanted, the kind of management structure he wanted, and more. He was now beginning to get some interviews, and he was feeling confident about the new prospects he was meeting.

Writing your wildest goals pays off. A study of Harvard alumni 10 years after graduation found that 83 percent had no specific business or personal goals, 14 percent had specific

goals, but had not written them, and 3 percent had specific goals that were written. The graduates with specific, but unwritten, goals were earning about THREE TIMES as much as those with no goals. And those with specific WRITTEN goals were earning 10 TIMES as much as those with no goals.

Simply, when we commit to writing or typing HOW we will succeed, we can readily visualize our success. Visualized success works because the mind can't tell the difference between an imagined experience and a real one. Our bodies respond to what our minds visualize as true. In short, what we think about, we bring about.

Commanding our minds to succeed is the secret to living life ON PURPOSE. Purposeful commitments propel us toward triumph.

18

3 Musts for Stress Free Work

You can satisfy others
while also satisfying yourself!

While speaking before a woman's forum, I was handed this saying: "A woman is like a teabag—you never know how strong she is until you get her in hot water." Women have the reputation of being steel magnolias. But actually, if we are really so strong, why are we the major consumers of antacids? Why don't we admit to being "angry," instead of politely saying we're "depressed" or "hurt"?

Depression is anger turned inward, directed at us by ourselves. That's not strength at all; it's passivity. The result of not achieving the success you long for causes stress—which can ultimately kill you.

Women are not alone in needing help in handling stress. More and more men are seeking me out for stress management techniques. At work, men and women alike are told that to get ahead is to get along. They think they should swallow their tongue, and swallow their Tums. Swallow and wallow.

At home, many people follow the same routine. According to the University of Michigan School of Public Health, swallowing your emotions can be dangerous. Their study found that swallowing anger toward a mate can double a person's risk of premature death.

The "Don't make waves" mantra at the office causes most people to follow the formula for peacemaking, pleasing, and placating. But that notion denies and defies their individuality. Ignoring who you are is painful and stressful. We don't need the advice of self-help gurus and shrinks to tell us that most of us have difficulty confronting. For years, Oprah Winfrey admitted confrontation is one of her own greatest flaws.

How can we mortals get our emotions out, clear our thoughts, cleanse our consciences, and win respect? Follow the 3 Musts for a Stress-Free Life. This prescription mandates that we must respond to life's crises, rather than react to them. It won't happen automatically all the time, but it certainly will happen when you remember what the necessary ingredients are.

Must #1
I SHALL EMPOWER MYSELF.

Many years ago, Gloria Steinem said that people waste too much time waiting for someone to take charge of their lives. While I was running a Management Optimization Seminar attended by mostly male executives, the managers bemoaned their boss for not promoting them and giving them raises.

When I asked whether their boss knew about their discontent, they said, "He *should* know!"

In reality, not one of them had shared their goals and aspirations with this superior. Time is life. Don't wait for someone to come along and give you a job, a raise, a promotion, or a break. Take the reins yourself.

We all have natural power. Look the part, feel the part, and be willing to discuss what you want. Project a Power Image™, which is the name of a very popular workshop I have conducted around the country. Empowered people demonstrate control over their lives—and attract people who help them achieve it.

Must #2
I WILL NEVER BE LIKED
IF I CAN'T RISK BEING DISLIKED.

Most people want respect, but have trouble giving up their need to be liked. Multitasking aside, most of us can only do one thing **effectively** at a time. If you're trying to accomplish a particular goal, forget whether people will approve or disapprove. Pursue the goal on your own, and gain respect for having achieved it when it's done.

The success sequence mandates respect first, and liking later. Risk being disliked, and state what makes you happy. You are entitled to your own feelings. If you require support, tell people honestly, "I need . . .," "I want . . .," "I feel . . .."

It's not a diminution of self to request backup. Whichever people in your life won't honor your goals are actually doing you a big favor, because they're clearly letting you know you can't count on them. And you can gracefully move on.

Must #3
WHAT I ACCEPT, I TEACH.

If you accept poor treatment from a boss or colleagues, you teach these people that it's okay to continue disregarding you. Confront adversity as soon as it strikes. As writer Somerset Maugham said, "When we refuse to accept anything but the very best, we very often get it."

Power is as power *does*. Power does as power *feels*. Power feels as power *thinks*. THINK these 3 musts, and ingrain them in your conscious mind. Then watch how your thoughts affect others' actions toward you.

What you give out, you'll get back. As you garner more recognition for your hard work, your stress will lessen, and you'll extend your life! What greater reward could you ask for?

19

Perfect Your Phone Charisma

Most listeners disengage after only 7 seconds.

Before making a business call, most people rehearse important words and phrases in their minds. But we usually don't prep for a magnetic style of presentation—and that's what counts most.

A startling 78 percent of the image you project on the phone depends on your voice: enunciation, tone, volume, rhythm, pitch, dialect, and rate of speech. Studies show that the actual words used on that impersonal device count for only 22 percent of our effectiveness.

In other words, *how* we say something is more important than *what* we say. And the way a listener receives our communication complicates the matter.

After the first 7 seconds, the listener is ready for a mental break. If you make it to the 15-second mark, your listener will begin to stereotype your ethnicity, personality, educational background, intelligence, upbringing, and class.

From all this information, the listener decides the kind of information to give you, his or her desired degree of involvement, how carefully to listen, and how much to trust you.

At the 30-second point, the listener has usually had enough. This is the length of the average media commercial, and the extent to which we as a culture have been conditioned to persevere at listening.

So, optimize the few crucial moments you have on the phone. Follow these 5 steps to telephone success.

Step #1
The Physical Positioning

Gather preparatory papers, connect to the necessary number, and probably most difficult, get through the gatekeeper whose job it is to prevent you from reaching your desired contact. Keep a sense of humor during this information-disseminating step.

I announced my name and professional title, Dr. Gilda Carle, to a client's receptionist. She seriously asked me, "Is 'doctor' your first name?" Another time, I said, "This is Dr. Gilda Carle to speak with Dr. John Smith." This silly secretary responded, "Are you his nurse?" If you don't appreciate the absurd humor, your seriousness will contaminate the information that needs to be sent.

Step #2
The Social Amenities

Small talk prior to addressing the reason for your call can smooth the way. "John, how are you doing?" "Mel, how's the weather now in Aspen?" "I hear your company is doing great work." These niceties pave the way for breaking the mood you find your listener in, and moving that listener into receptivity mode.

Step #3
The Main Topic

Of course, this is the only reason you are making the call. But people who avoid the first two steps and go right into the main topic are criticized as being cold, and their messages are summarily dismissed.

Step #4
The Social Conclusion

Some graceful ways to close a conversation are, "Say hi to your boss," or "Enjoy the rest of the day" or "Let me know when I can help you further." You always want to leave the conversation on a light and positive note so this is the way you can be remembered.

Step #5
The Physical Re-positioning

After you disconnect, follow up with personal notes, letters, or calls to someone else who must get involved. Do this follow-up while the information is still fresh in your mind.

If you make 10 phone calls, count 20 positioning aspects (the Physical Positioning at the beginning and the Physical Re-positioning at the end), 20 social aspects (the Social Amenities at the beginning and the Social Conclusion at the end), and 10 main topics. That's 50 pieces of telephone etiquette that account for your precious time.

You'll also need 9 momentum-rebuilders of 20 minutes each, which can take an additional 180 minutes, or 3 full hours! Is it any wonder you are exhausted after all this talk?

Moreover, since 75 percent of all business calls are not completed with the right person on the first try, some of these steps will need to be repeated several times.

What appears to be so cost-efficient on face value can turn out as prohibitively expensive if it doesn't work effectively. If you want to line up successful business, be sure all your lines of communication are being optimized.

20

Use This Blueprint as an Interviewer

Successful interviews require six sequential stages

Most people take interviewing skills for granted. Actually, the process is a dance initiated by one partner and followed by another, each taking turns as leader and follower. A successful employment interview requires refining the interactions of the communicators with careful preparations and protocols.

The objective is for you and your applicant to arrive at a level of rapport that can glide into a mutually beneficial work relationship. Success for the applicant means getting the desired job offer; success for you means finding the most qualified candidate for the position.

It is to everyone's benefit for a "fit" to occur among the applicant, the organization, and you. This fit should encompass 3 areas:

1. The candidate's specific job-related skills and experience

2. His or her general intelligence and aptitude

3. His or her personality and attitude

Once the objectives are established, the interview can begin. The process consists of 6 sequential stages, each evolving from the one before it. It is your responsibility as interviewer to orchestrate and control the setting, rhythm, pace, and timing of each stage.

Stage 1
PREPARATION

Josh was a well-qualified job applicant, one his interviewer wanted to court. This was his fourth and hopefully final interview with this company.

The candidate had traveled two hours to make this appointment, so he was naturally turned off by the interviewer's casual question, "So…tell me about yourself" during this crucial final interview after three previous successful ones. It was obvious the interviewer had not taken the time to peruse Josh's resume before this face-to-face meeting. Now it seemed this interviewer wanted to engage in meaningless small talk to camouflage his lack of preparation. Although the interview got better over the next half hour, Josh vowed never to step foot into that company again. Everyone lost out.

Whenever you invite an applicant for an interview, consider him or her as an honored guest. You have an obligation to prepare for that meeting and to make your guest feel welcome. Failing to prepare is preparing to fail.

Don't waste everyone's valuable time or reputation if your intention is not whole-hearted.

Preparation requires designing specific questions in advance, based on the candidate's written credentials, to target appropriate information you want to derive. Not only will such preparation save time, it will also impress the candidate about how you and your company value people.

Types of Questions to Ask

The questions you design may consist of either *closed-ended* or *open-ended* formats. Close-ended questions begin with words like, "Who?," "When?," "Where?," "Which?," "Are?," and "Did?"

These kinds of questions invite short or one-word responses, and therefore end an interaction before it begins. At that point, you may find yourself straining for other questions to prompt further discussion, but already, an uncomfortable and unprofessional atmosphere has emerged.

To keep conversation moving, prepare open-ended formats using, "How?," "Why?," and "In what way?" These encourage discussion and explanation.

The more the candidate talks, the more you will learn about his or her talents and personality—and the better you will be able to make a judgment. Incorporate the "two ears to one mouth" ratio: Listen to the candidate speak more than you do. Then formulate insights not only from the words the candidate offers, but also from the feelings behind the words.

Plan specific questions around 3 types:

The Direct Question: This requests specific information in a straightforward manner.

*   "How did your academic credentials at Carnegie Mellon prepare you for your last job as a civil engineer ?"

*   "Which of your personal strengths do you think will be the most beneficial to the position you seek in our company?"

    Open-ended formats are structured to get the applicant to communicate freely. However, if the candidate rambles on for too long, interrupt with a closed-ended design that requires a yes or no response.

The Indirect Question: Although it does not demand a direct answer, this is a statement that implies a question and encourages discussion.

*   "I'm interested to know how your last position at Citibank prepared you for this position at our company."

- "You must have had little personal time while working during the day and attending graduate school at night."

The Leading Question: This is a direct question indicating that a specific answer is preferred. But becareful! Because the respondent may be aware that you prefer only one right answer, his or her effort to preserve the relationship may preclude total honesty.

- "Wouldn't going to graduate school for seven years motivate a person to finally get his degree?"

- "Isn't it unique for a woman, so early in her career, to have had three major positions as Vice President?"

Avoid using the double question where two questions are asked in immediate succession. The double question confuses the applicant because one question is usually open, while the other is usually closed.

- "Where was your office? Was it far from here?"

- "How would you handle a hostile employee? Would you let him get by for a while, or immediately confront his behavior?"

- "Describe your boss's functions. What was her title?"

While probing questions can reveal a candidate's value to a company, avoid topics that violate the law. Subjects like religion, age, sex, and marital or family status, physical handicaps, arrest record, and financial affairs are taboo.

When you set up the process with thoroughly prepared questions, the tone of the interview begins with seriousness and respect. Then the 5 steps that follow can flow naturally and productively.

Stage 2
BUILDING RAPPORT
IN THE FIRST FEW MINUTES

Interviews are usually anxiety producing for most job applicants. You will get a better "read'" of your guest's employment potential by quickly putting him or her at ease and establishing rapport as soon as possible. This involves simple and casual "schmoozing."

Schmoozing is an art. It delicately determines how much further an interaction should go, while also setting the stage for the meat of the interview that follows.

Small talk is not for the impatient interviewer; it takes time to pace your candidate through this seemingly inconsequential banter. But when your candidate is relaxed and at ease, your reward will be "free information" that reveals the true person with whom you are conversing, and his or her potential to fit with your organization. What you must do during this process is listen very carefully to what is said, but especially to what is omitted.

ONE-UP STRATEGIES

The small talk process involves 3 steps:

1.   Exchange impersonal pleasantries about topics such as the weather or traffic. Avoid politics, religion, or sex, since they could lead to disagreement, and even a lawsuit.

2.   Pool common interests by discussing similar backgrounds and hobbies. You can easily establish this commonality after combing the applicant's resume.

3.   Open channels for further communication relevant to the interview. Be sure the topics include only three: you, the applicant, or the situation.

Talking about yourself rarely stimulates conversation. An applicant, nervous to begin with, will probably be at a loss as to how to respond to the stranger who is also an evaluator.

In the same vein, initially discussing the applicant is likely to put him or her on the defensive, which is an uncomfortable way to begin. Therefore, the least anxiety-provoking topic for small talk is the position for which the applicant has applied.

In discussing the position, once again choose from 3 approaches:

a) Voice an opinion.

b) State a fact.

  c) Ask a question.

The first two possibilities, voicing an opinion or stating a fact, are one-way communication techniques that require no feedback from the applicant, and thereby provide no information. So, the best way to stimulate conversation is the last possibility:
Ask a question.

Consciously and specifically select from either closed-ended or open-ended formats to derive the information you need.

For example, these closed-ended formats, "Did you save your company money?" and "When did you institute your new computer system?" rapidly derived facts from Alice who was interviewing for the job of Sales Manager. But that was as far as they went. Her response to the first question was "Yes," and her response to the second was "Three years ago." Period.

In contrast, these open-ended formats, "How did you save your last company money?" and "Why did you institute a new system of cold calling?" filled the interviewer in on background details that had not been discussed earlier, while it also stimulated additional conversation.

Stage 3
SET THE STRUCTURE OF THE MEETING

You, as orchestrator of this interview process, must let the applicant know the roadmap you will be following.

When describing the structure of the interview, use the candidate's name to sharpen rapport: "Pat (Do you mind if I use your first name?), our meeting this morning will last 45 minutes. It will be divided into two parts.

In the first part, I want to learn about your work experience, academic credentials, and the personal strengths you can offer our company. In the second part, I would like to hear about your interest in our company and answer your questions. I hope you don't mind that I will be taking notes for my records."

This preface shows the candidate that you have a specific blueprint that you're following, and it also lets him or her know that you have already invested time in getting to know this person, at least through his or her resume.

Stage 4
INFORMATION-GATHERING

Now that you have targeted specific questions during the preparatory steps, it is time to gather the details you need.

Too many interviewers talk more than they listen, and they come away with too little information on which to base a fair decision. You may use any or all the methods of questioning described above, provided the focus remains on the candidate and not you.

You need to ensure the applicant's full involvement in the process. Involving him or her requires the use of the 80/20 Rule, talking only 20 percent of the time, while listening 80 percent.

While applying this Rule, choose from any or all of the following 4 strategies for Active Listening:

1. The Mm-Hm Response: This regulates the give-and-take of conversation as you signal that the applicant still has the floor. Your response may be nonverbal (head nodding) or verbal ("Mm-hm, I see;" "That's   interesting;" "Really?").

   Research shows that interviewers who ask questions that last 5 or 6 seconds usually get responses in the 30- to 40-second range. But those who use the Mm-Hm Response increase candidates' replies to 50 to 60 seconds.

   The Mm-Hm Response not only encourages increased candidate reaction; it also gives you additional time to consider the response, before deciding to probe further.

2. Restatement of the Content: Repeat or summarize statements expressed by the respondent. This Re-statement confirms your understanding of what the speaker said, while also inviting him or her to clarify misperceived information.

3. Reflection of Feelings: Verbalize your perception of the emotions expressed by the applicant: "It seems, Robert, that when you speak about your last position, you become upset." Or, "You appear to have enjoyed your last management position." This Active Listening strategy invites the can didate to expand on what he or she said, and/or clarify your perceptions.

4.   Use of Silence: It is up to you as the interview or chestrator not to fill each moment of silence with idle chatter. The respondent needs time to process your questions and to organize thoughts to frame ananswer. Even after he or she responds to your last question, allow about 6 seconds for this person to digest the content.

Stage 5
SELL THE POSITION
AND THE COMPANY

Once your candidate demonstrates potential as a future employee, you will want to promote the organization to entice him or her to work there. One of your candidate's outstanding qualities will probably be the obvious effort made before the interview to discover the company's strong points.

Continue your role as gracious host by asking if the candidate has further questions about the company that have not already been answered. Review the advantages the company offers, and invite him or her to tour the operation and to meet with and talk to people who may be future colleagues. Provide a packet of materials about the company. Because you have Actively Listened to your candidate's needs and motives, shape your sales pitch to what you think is important to him or her.

Stage 6
THE CLOSE

This last stage should end on a note of good will. If

the candidate is not right for the job, nevertheless finish the interview on a positive note. An applicant treated equitably may recommend another applicant better suited for the position. Or, at least, the candidate will not speak ill of the organization or you.

Believe it or not, you may find yourself in a similar position of job seeking somewhere down the road, and may need to draw on your good reputation built years earlier.

Tom had experienced a very difficult interview process from a nasty man who seemed to dislike him from the moment he walked in the door. The interviewer was less than gracious, and his snide personal remarks caused Tom to end the interview abruptly, nonetheless leaning over and extending his hand, as he said, "Thank you for your time. I don't think this is the job for me." Then he left.

That might have been the end of the story, but about six years later, Tom, now a vice president of a huge conglomerate, was in the position of interviewing candidates himself for one of his assistants. He almost fell over when the nasty man who had interviewed him years earlier walked through the door. Although Mr. Nasty's credentials were impeccable, the memory of the experience Tom had had with him killed any hope of the pair engaging in a future together.

As your candidate prepares to leave, map out the next steps that will be taken, and how soon your company will be in contact.

The Meaning Behind All Interviews

The aim of an interview is to get at crucial information as quickly as possible to determine a candidate's employment potential for your firm. There's no need to be nervous, because interviews are merely formalized conversations.

The better equipped you are at probing for key data, the more you will sharpen your communication skills, proficiencies that cut across all aspects of your life and future success.

21

Deal Optimistically
with Job Rejection

The issue you perceive is never the real issue.

When I first started my company, I was an academician with an advanced degree in book knowledge, and little else. No one in the business world knew me. What is a new businessperson to do? Without a script of lessons such as these in self-promotion and networking, how unprepared I was for what was to follow!

Either by phone or in person, I'd introduce myself, tell the listener what I did, and invariably get either a cool, "No, thank you," a tepid, "We're not interested," or a heated, "We're never in need of your services." Goodbye, get lost, good riddance. I was so depressed that I began to average just one cold (frigid!) call a day.

Life truly is just a schoolroom. Most people internalize a job rejection as a personal assault. It seems that for too many, the meaning of being accepted is their measure of how lovable they are. And for the all-too-vulnerable, it is the test question that decides their final grade.

Sure, it's natural to want to feel accepted and included. But if so much emphasis is placed on it, the fear of not getting this love can create emotional paralysis, and in turn sabotage upward mobility. So, what is a rejected job seeker to do next?

1.   Understand that you will never be loved if you can't risk being disliked. Shutting down after a rejection puts you out of the running for positions for which you are probably better suited.

2.   Feel to deal and deal to heal. In other words, feel the depths of your rejection fears, understand the meaning, and accept reality as it is. Not everyone will always love us. Consciously commit not to allow rejection to bring you down. In other words, deal and ye shall heal!

3.   Be philosophical and optimistic. That will give you the strength to consciously formulate positive thought. For example, the negative impact of the statement, "Why would The Jones Company want to hire me, anyway?" will set your mind into an "I'm-not-good-enough" state. The first person you allow to negate you—and that's usu ally you—can set off a chain re-action that will threaten future success. Don't believe me? Well, would YOU choose to hang around a downer?

It takes 15 to 100 billion brain neurons for us to make each choice. The brain does not judge the positivity or negativity of the choices we choose. With positive self-talk, the words "praise" and "blame" are correctly interpreted to mean the same—as mere inconsequential opinions of others. Ultimately, your continued sustenance is derived from WITHIN YOU, not from the shaky and changeable people outside.

One corporate president I was coaching was upset over the hostile takeover of the company he had founded. After going on and on about how unjust the situation was, I asked him to answer the following 3 questions:

• What do you think about this?

• What would you like to think about this?

• What do you choose to think about this?

From his responses, he realized that his real issue was not about losing his company, but about personally feeling rejected. I asked him about the status of another company he was considering to buy. In describing its corporate culture, he worried about the struggle he would have in being accepted by that company's difficult employees. We quickly uncovered that for this man, business success was totally about feeling loved.

Once we discussed this, and the genesis of these feelings, he was ready to move away from his feelings and on to tangible achievement. He chose to feel his fear, deal with it, and heal himself of irrational pain by *choosing* to think differently. That was the last of my 3 questions this man answered. He proceeded to his next business successfully.

This corporate president had learned a great deal. He had thought he had ego issues around being replaced; instead, he learned that his issues centered on feeling accepted—and once he uncovered this, he was able to let these damaging feelings go.

As you've read throughout this book, the issue you perceive is never the real issue. Look beyond the obvious to discover every issue's true meaning.

Choosing in advance to believe you are already liked and accepted programs you to avoid feeling sorry for yourself. Then you can move on to performing your tasks well. Choosing in advance to believe you DE-SERVE success programs you to create a positive destiny.

Make every thought an encouraging one. As you do your business, during good days and bad days, the next time you feel rejected, tell yourself, "It's not a personal rejection; it's just a refusal to do business—*at this time*."

The word "No" should never be interpreted as "No forever." Instead, change its meaning to simply, "Not yet." Then keep pressing forward. Positivity is contagious. Once you state it, you'll create it.

22

Beware of the Success Blocker

Too many heart attacks
occur at 9am Monday morning at work.

The disease now sweeping our workforce is industrial-strength malaise. It causes employees to stay stuck in their jobs, even though they can't stand them. It is therefore not surprising that the majority of heart attacks occur after a relaxing weekend, at 9am Monday morning at that dreaded job.

Most of us have swallowed the fairy tale myth that assures a fictitious "happily-ever-after" ending to a life's linear journey that is, in reality, anything but linear.

By now you know that few rises on the success ladder are straight up to the top. What we really find are many broken rungs, turnarounds, and back steps before we reach each sought after goal.

This is how the fantasy works. We think we've found the job of our dreams, our "Prince Charming." We trust this career coup will challenge us and also pay the bills. We assume we'll be rewarded in conjunction with our output. We work hard and wait—for recognition, promotions, and salary increases. Nothing happens.

We are frustrated that our alleged savior hasn't kept the promise it doesn't even know it made. At some point, for some reason, we had transformed into the proverbial passive employee, no longer controlling our own career, but waiting instead for someone to save us. No one comes. When we see what we haven't gotten *after all this time*, we internalize anger or we become sick . . .

Each time an employee complains to me about having been passed over for something, I respond, "YOU create your future." My response doesn't especially sit well with people conditioned to believe that everything is up to the boss or the company—and not to them.

I explain the concept of Victim Mentality, where people pass their power to someone less capable than they are. Traditionally, it has always been women who have waited for the immortal "Prince Charming" to sweep us off our feet, take care of us, and make us happy.

But now, more and more men are seeking help for their stress and anger. Many are furious because they didn't get what they thought they were entitled to. Most times, they had never shared their feelings and goals with the people who were in the position of rewarding their efforts.

When I asked a group of angry male managers if they had told their boss what their goals were, they replied, "He should know." Really? These days, the boss is lucky if he can hold on to his own job.

The fairy tale myth has taught us to wait instead of communicate. Of course, it's common knowledge that "difficult" employees who make unwieldy demands are the first to be let go. And some organizations shut down whole divisions just to get rid of a few problem "children." But keeping mum is the exact opposite, and it's also a sure-fire way to die a slow death and lose your job anyway.

There is a middle ground between the waiting and remaining mum and the overly outspoken disgruntled employee. It's called "communicating with grace," and it consists of only 3 steps:

1. Converse with your boss during a stress-free time, when you can freely share your goals. The goals you set will plot the rewards you get.

2. Specifically ask your boss, "How can I get from Point A to Point B—with your help?" In this way, you're not waiting for something to happen. Also, you're not seeming to be angry or dis gruntled. You're simply sharing your mission statement and asking for support from someone capable of making it a reality.

3. Listen, listen, listen. Perhaps your boss has reser vations about your upward mobility. If so, hear him or her out—without interruption. Perhaps

your boss never thought you were interested in a job other than the one you have. Perhaps he or she was waiting for YOU to initiate a discussion of your goals.

Many bosses tell me they will not offer someone a promotion if the person doesn't ASK FOR IT. They say they want to be sure the person is motivated enough to carry out his or her dreams.

If you don't ask, you certainly won't get. But if you do ask, and you still don't get, that's important information for you to have. It will kick you in the butt to find a more rewarding environment that appreciates your skills and talents.

Whatever you do, don't wait for Prince Charming to do it for you. Consider yourself your own Prince, and initiate your goals NOW.

23

Strategize as a Job Applicant

Consider yourself a product you must market.

When you are invited to interview for a job, be confident that the prospective employer sees a satisfactory match between the job requirements and your resume's credentials. The company would probably be just as comfortable employing you as it would any of the other invited candidates.

The issue that will determine the final outcome is the congruence or "fit" of personality, attitudes, and values between you and the interviewer, or, more specifically, between you and the company, because that's who the interviewer reflects.

Until the offer is in hand, knowing how to secure a job can be as important as knowing how to *perform* it. While a resume reviews what you have done in your professional career, the interviewer asks you how it was accomplished. A 60-minute interview can land or lose a potential opportunity.

Now the moment of truth arrives with your ability to persuade the prospective employer face-to-face that you will make a better employee than the other applicants. Such persuasion requires your ability to sell.

For many professionals, the word "sell" has a negative connotation, especially when they think of selling themselves. What also comes to mind is the used car salesman or the pushy, fast-talking huckster interested only in grabbing a customer's money. Even the dictionary defines "selling" as "cheating," "tricking," and "betraying."

Selling is mistakenly thought of as something done to people, usually against their wills. Yet, today, whether engineer or entrepreneur, everybody sells. Everyone needs to influence decision makers to accept their ideas, services, or products.

Selling is especially necessary for job seekers. But it's been made so much eassier through Social Media. Of course, much preparation is required to ensure that an application results in a job offer. Sellers must convince buyers that they have the talent, the know-how, and the technology that sets them apart from the rest.

According to one recruitment specialist, 47 percent of the shortcomings of candidates involve their failure to research a firm in advance and to prepare for the interview. (The Internet makes research very simple.) Another 230 percent of candidates' errors concerned their failure to "sell" their strengths and accomplishments. (Social Media outlets give everyone great practice in this skill.)

These findings suggest that nearly 70 percent of an interview requires skills beyond technical training, education, experience, and ability. This large percentage often offends professionals who have spent much time developing the talent for their specific field, but have invested little time in the skills reviewed in this book.

Every candidate must show himself or herself as outstanding when compared with the competition. And this is the true meaning of selling.

Don't accept the negative implications of the term "selling." Instead, view yourself as a product and your potential employer as a customer. As a product, avoid reiterating the major points outlined on your resume. That would be analogous to an auto company outlining to customers the basic parts of its automobiles as four wheels, an engine, brakes, and seats.

Job applicants often make the mistake of enumerating these key resume points when they are asked to describe their backgrounds. If the interviewer had reviewed their resume, this would be unnecessary repetition. Besides, once the list has been reiterated, it is the interviewer who must independently probe a candidate's potential worth to the organization.

One sales manager taught his trainees, "Don't sell me a refrigerator; sell me the solution to keeping my food cold." In other words, the salesperson sells the benefits of a product, benefits the consumer would not want to be without.

Along the same lines, you must *show how the company will benefit by hiring you instead of the other applicants* who have looked sufficiently attractive on paper or the computer screen to warrant an interview. Where should you begin?

Homework Impresses

Products don't just happen; they are designed to fill a specific need that has already been determined. Attach a letter of application to your resume that emphasizes how your strengths fit the job requirements. Key terms from the company's website should be repeated and highlighted in the letter to make it easier for the screener to match your qualifications with the job.

When you receive an invitation for an interview, based on your letter of application and your resume, the interviewer has already decided that his organization is interested in the skills you appear to offer. But now it is up to you to discover pertinent information about the company, so you can discuss the congruence of its requirements and your capabilities.

This is where it's imperative for you to feel comfortable discussing your personal strengths and limitations, because these will certainly be questioned. Self knowledge, as well as knowledge of the potential buyer, gives you an advantage for selling the interviewer on your ability to match what the company is seeking.

Besides exploring the company thoroughly, if you are invited to travel to an unfamiliar community or part of town, arrive early, and read a local newspaper to become conversant about community affairs. Displaying your familiarity with neighborhood events will pay big dividends during your interview.

The homework you do may seem arduous and time-consuming. But the knowledge you gain will help you demonstrate a sincere interest in working for the company, and a dedication to getting the job.

HOW TO ENHANCE YOUR INTERVIEW

After researching a particular organization, understand that there are three elements to consider: 1. the interviewer's focus, 2. your objective, and 3. how you intend to get your information across. These three elements require you to be selling at your best, as you follow a 4-part approach.

Be prepared that your **Interviewer's Focus** might begin from a point of apathy, and proceed towards an attitude of "How will this person enhance this organization?" The 4 steps of the Interviewer's Focus are:

1. Ho Hum . . .
2. What Can This Applicant Offer?
3. For Example?
4. So What?

Acknowledging the Interviewer's Focus, the **Applicant's Objective** must be to respond to the Interviewer through your own creative 4 steps that:

ONE-UP STRATEGIES

1. Engage
2. Emphasize
3. Envision
4. Enlist

The most efficient **Applicant's Method** to employ follows 4 deliberate and succinct steps that:

1. Relate
2. Communicate
3. Illustrate
4. Activate

HOW THIS WORKS

Part I
ENGAGE the Interviewer

Engaging the interviewer at the outset sets the stage for all that will follow. It's not unusual for interviewers who have been consecutively meeting and greeting many applicants to regard each as a "Ho Hum . . ." routine. Don't take this personally.

Instead, take the initiative to Engage the interviewer's attention immediately, creating good will through receptive body language, focused eye contact, and a light, but sincere attitude. All these elements should *Relate* a blend of personal vulnerability and professional seriousness.

Since you currnetly lack the position power that accom-panies being part of this organization, you must rely on your personal power. Personal power requires you to find an assertive way of relating to the interviewer that is natural and nonthreatening.

Professionalism extends beyond clothing to attitude and manner. It may be hard for professionals to believe, but body language accounts for 55 percent of the impression they make.

Image begins with a firm and confident handshake. But energy and vitality can also be projected through such action words as "establish, "develop," "participate," "initiate," and "innovate." These terms suggest a person who gets things accomplished.

You can build interviewing muscle if you practice selling yourself in 30-second time slots, similar to media commercials with which everyone is familiar. Also, keep in mind that a listener may take a mental vacation after only 7 measly seconds.

Although an interview may be scheduled to last for 60 minutes, it may be the first 60 seconds during which judgments are formulated to determine if you have a future with that company.

Part of preparing a 30-second commercial on yourself requires organizing and focusing key points concisely, eliminating unnecessary information. Thirty seconds flies by quickly. You can study television and radio advertisements to understand how professionals sell their benefits in minute time frames.

Part II
EMPHASIZE the Match
between Your Qualifications
and the Job's Requirements

After you have captured your interviewer's interest, it is time to sell the *benefits that set you apart from the crowd.* Now that you have successfully nudged the interviewer from the "Ho Hum . . ." fence of apathy and indecision, address the interviewer's main concern: "How do this candidate's qualifications match the requirements of this position in our company?"

At this point, *Communicate* with your host by appealing to the company's needs and interests according to what you uncovered through doing your homework. The word "communication" emphasizes a "communion" of ideas and philosophies indicating the appropriateness of the "fit" between you and your listener.

One means of accomplishing this communion is by asking relevant and incisive questions. Author James Thurber wrote, "It is better to know some of the questions than to know all the answers." As part of your homework, prepare 10 complex questions in advance to Enlighten the interviewer that you are familiar with the history and goals of the organization.

For example, "I know your company has recently switched to XYZ computer technology, but that some of your projects have been discontinued. Could you explain how your focus has changed in the past few years?" This question is open-ended (See Chapter 20: "Use This Blueprint as an Interviewer" for a further explanation about open-ended and close-ended questions), and it provides an opportunity for the interviewer to explain information not available in other sources. It also shows the impressive homework you did in advance.

While the interviewer is responding to the questions you pose, your listening skills and your enthusiasm are being evaluated. Be careful to allow your interviewer to complete each thought without interruption. The rule of thumb for Active Listening is to use the ratio of two ears to one mouth. As best you can, match your own energy level with that of the interviewer to enhance the chemistry between the two of you.

Just as it is important to prepare 10 questions you might want to ask the interviewer, also create 10 questions you would hate being asked. For example, one young lawyer was asked, "Are you married?" Having rehearsed for such a possibility in advance, and recognizing that she wanted the job and did not want to quote chapter and verse from the Equal Employment Opportunity Commission, she naively responded with, "What do you mean?"

The interviewer knew that he had overstepped his boundaries, so he covered his tracks by explaining that the job required much travel, and he was looking out for the stability of every candidate's family life. However, he immediately dropped the question. By formulating possible responses to objectionable questions in advance, you can be equipped for a difficult meeting.

Part III
ENVISION for Your Interviewer

Selling your credentials by just telling your interviewer about them isn't enough. People only remember a paltry 10 percent of the information they receive through words.

Showing your points is a better approach to use to instill your information. It employs a stronger pitch for your accomplishments, and it provides the opportunity for an interviewer to remember a larger 25 percent of the information you display.

For example, you may state that as Chief Engineer at Relco Corporation, you were credited for having saved your department $20,000. That alone is impressive. However, if you display reports, company statements, statistics, charts, articles, or brochures to which you contributed, the visuals will remain in the interviewer's memory long after the meeting is over.

These visuals serve to define the *hows* of your accomplishments as they demonstrate your transfer of problems into solutions. Finding an employee who can convert issues into non-issues is a greatly sought after commodity.

Part IV
ENLIST the Interviewer to Follow Up

Now that you have posed the significant benefits and presented the "fit" between yourself and the potential employer, a conclusion is in order. Although you have impressed your host, communicated your congruent philosophies, and illustrated the *hows* of former performance, the interviewer may still skeptically respond with "So What?"

Remember that the interviewer's selection ability is also being assessed by the rest of the company. Don't take his or her "So What?" personally. Instead, lookat this as your final chance to make a lasting impression. The objective is now to Enlist your interviewer to act and select you.

Similar to a successful salesperson who knows when to close a deal, now is your chance to request the interviewer's action or reaction. *In other words, actually ask for the job!* A passive job seeker may leave an impression of disinterest.

In contrast, be assertive, make your last pitch, summarize with cogent reasons why the company should hire you, and leave with an upbeat comment and a smile.

The image you present at parting will be lasting. Be sure you feel in control. If you followed all the steps to Enhancing Your Interview, but omit this last crucial Enlistment step, the deal has not yet been completed and sealed.

Make your final image a positive one. Activate the interviewer to choose YOU. But even if things don't work out as you would like, don't give up.

Arnold applied for the job of Associate Professor at an impressive Midwest university. He went through a rigorous interview process, flying to the location for interviews at least three times, and thinking that he had interviewed well. But when push came to shove, it was not he they selected for the job.

He continued interviewing for other positions in other universities around the country, settled on one he thought was all right, and took it. He remained there for two years, and was seemingly happy.

Then one day, he received a call from the Dean at the Midwest university at which he had originally interviewed. It seemed the person who they hired for that position had a family problem and needed to return east. The Dean who had interviewed Arnold two long years earlier remembered his qualifications and how impressive he was. Now this same Dean wanted to re-consider his candidacy.

Arnold jumped at the chance. The last time I ran into him, Arnold told me he had become tenured at this university, and had been a full professor there for the past 12 years!

Delays may not necessarily be denials. No matter where you go, always leave behind a piece of your positivity. It will never be forgotten.

24

Find the Success
in Every Silver Lining

There is always sun beneath the shade.

Within a matter of months, Jen had a new husband, a new job, and a new place to live. It did not take her long to discover that one of her choices, her new job, had not been thoroughly researched before she took it. At first, she did what most people do when things go bad: she complained . . . but remained . . . miserable.

Jen's misery continued for a few more months until the stomach ailments she was having began to spill over into her relationship with her new spouse. When she came to see me, she was pretty desperate for a solution. I shared with her my philosophy about coping with obstacles: When something happens TO us, it really happens FOR us. Jen's most important job was now to explore what possible good might lie beneath her unfulfilling work.

Through many coaching sessions, Jen uncovered a hidden desire to change careers altogether. She realized that she was tired and burned out from having performed the same duties, albeit in different organizations, for over a decade.

During the next few months, she did extensive research into a number of companies whose bottom lines were in the red. She had always felt she had a natural ability to creatively crunch numbers in a new way.

She interviewed with each company she had researched, and she was offered several jobs. The one she chose was an opportunity she had never dreamed possible. She admitted later that if not for the clouds, she would never have pursued a more colorful rainbow.

As ironic as this seems, a truth about difficulties is that things that give us the most grief often do us the most good. Think of someone at work who made you miserable, and in some peculiar way, was finally responsible for your moving onward and upward. Rather than curse that person for his or her actions toward you, thank that person for spurring you on!

Beneath every cloud is a silver lining. Take the Silver Lining Test below and discover if you can see beyond the fog.

The Silver Living Test

Answer True or False to each of the following questions:

1.   Good luck is important in life.

2.   When someone disappoints or upsets me, I aim to get even.

3.   I begin every relationship with distrust, until proven otherwise.

Scoring: If you marked 1 – 3 Trues, you're IN THE CLOUDS.

Explanations

1.   FALSE. While we usually can't help the circumstances that happen TO us, it is WE who determine how to respond. Being in the right place at the time is entirely up us. We create our luck an we create our destiny.

2.   FALSE. "Getting even" invests our energies in street-fighting with another person, rather than in achieving our goals. When an opponent is not acting up to par, get out of his or her way and wish that person good luck. Then get on with your life. Every moment you drop away from your own agenda puts your power in the hands of someone else.

3.   FALSE. What we give out, we get back. This is not to suggest that you should be naively trusting when you hardly know someone. During the beginning of every relationship, be speculative and tentative. But out-and-out distrust only be gets distrust in return. Instead of negativity, as

the song lyric goes, "Try a little ten-derness."
The tenderness you reap in return may surprise you.

So, rather than automatically interpreting a cloud as in-stant hardship, seek the silver living beneath its surface. Never ask, "Why is this happening to me?" Instead, ask, "What am I supposed to learn from this?" It's the old 80/20 Iceberg Rule: You only get to see 20 percent of reality, while 80 percent is hidden beneath the icy waters. Think the words "silver lining" as you search for as much of the 80 percent as you can find.

Also recognize that silver is superior to other substanc-es, because it conducts heat and electricity. So, seek the heat and electricity that's been absent from your life until now. Exude your personal radiance. The sunshine will eventually come out if you're willing to get in from the storm.

CONCLUSION

Business schools are deliberately set up to teach the nuts and bolts of leadership and management. And in that, they usually do a good job. One of the things they teach is that there is a bifurcation between the task at hand and the people who perform the task.

But most curricula tend to stop there. Just as other institutions of professional skill building, what is accented in business school programs is how to best perform a task. What is omitted are the people skills of those that need to drive the leaders and managers to perform exceptionally.

I have taught thousands of very book-bright MBA students who turned out not to have a clue when it came to understanding how to work with people. When they return to me with questions of what went wrong, or hire me to assess their corporate dysfunction, my findings always point to people issues.

I hope you are now more aware of the edge you can derive and apply when you master these skills. You have the upper hand because of your new insights. I would enjoy hearing your success stories at DrGilda.com. Knock 'em dead!

***

Dr. Gilda Carle (Ph.D.) is an internationally known management consultant, relationship educator, author, business school Professor Emerita, product spokesperson, and media personality. She conducts Lunch-and-Learns at major corporations, delivers keynote and motivational speeches, and provides Personal Coaching online, on the phone, and on email throughout the world. By uniquely integrating self-worth principles with net worth strategies, she is renowned for quickly raising the bottom line.

She is also President of Country Cures® (**www.CountryCures.org**), a non-profit educational charity she developed to provide Homeless Female Veterans with Empowerment Skills Training. Her programs distinctively use Country Music to save the lives of these SHEroes, along with those of their children and communities. For this unusual work, Dr. Gilda has earned the title "Country Music Doctor."

Having successfully fused personal relationship essentials with business achievement, she has authored 17 mass market relationship books, including "Don't Bet on the Prince!" (a test question on "Jeopardy!"), "How to WIN When Your Mate Cheats" (literary award winner from London Book Festival), and for teens and millennials, "Don't Lie on Your Back for a Guy Who Doesn't Have Yours," with its companion, "My Rants & Ramblings Journal."

She wrote the weekly "30-Second Therapist" column for the Today Show, the "Ask Dr. Gilda" column for Match.com, she was the relationship expert on TV's

Sally Jessy Raphael show, and every other national TV talk and news show, and she has conducted Relationship Wellness training for Columbia University Medical Center.

Dr. Gilda hosted MTV Online's "Love Doc," she was the therapist in HBO's Emmy Award winner, "Telling Nicholas" featured on Oprah, where she guided a family to tell their 7-year-old that his mom died in the World Trade Center on 9/11, she was the TV host for Fox's "Dr. Gilda" show pilot, and she hosts TV shows on Trinity Broadcasting Network. Her popular website is **www.DrGilda.com**

***

MASS MARKET BOOKS BY DR. GILDA

Dr. Gilda's Self-Worth Series
-- "I'm Worth Loving! Here's Why."
-- "Ask for What You Want—AND GET IT!
-- "How to Be a Worry-Free Woman"

Dr. Gilda's Relationship Series
--8 Steps to a Sizzling Marriage
--8 Tips to Understand the Opposite Sex
--10 Questions Single Women Should Never
   Ask & 10 They Should
--10 Signs of a Cheater-to-Be

Dr. Gilda's Fidelity Series
--Why Your Cheater Keeps Cheating—And
   You're Still There!

ONE-UP STRATEGIES

--How to Cope with the Cheater You Love—and WIN

--99 Prescriptions for Fidelity: Your Rx for Trust

***

<u>ALSO</u>

--Don't Bet on the Prince! How to Have the Man *You Want by Betting on Yourself*

--Don't Lie on Your Back for a Guy Who Doesn't Have Yours

--My Rants & Ramblings Journal (companion to "Don't Lie on Your Back for a Guy Who Doesn't Have Yours")

***

Benefit from Dr. Gilda's
one-on-one Advice & Coaching
www.DrGilda.com

www.ingramcontent.com/pod-product-compliance
Lightning Source LLC
Chambersburg PA
CBHW060910280326
41934CB00007B/1256